PREPARING FOR COMPETITION WEIGHTLIFTING

PREPARING FOR COMPETITION WEIGHTLIFTING

DAVID WEBSTER

SBL SPRINGFIELD BOOKS LIMITED

Published by **Springfield Books Limited,**
Norman Road, Denby Dale, Huddersfield
HD8 8TH, England

Copyright © 1986 David Webster

ISBN 0 947655 11 5 (cased)
    0 947655 09 3 (paperback)

Design: Hand and Beever
Typesetting: Netherwood Dalton & Co Limited
Printed and bound in England by
The Bath Press

Webster, David, *1928-*
    Preparing for competition weightlifting.
    1. Weight lifting
    I.Title
    796.4'1   GV546.3

Contents

The Helping Hands

The author wishes to record his sincere thanks to lifters and officials who have helped with research and in various other ways. Particular thanks are due to George Kirkley, an experienced and talented weightlifting photographer who took most of the photographs for this publication and is a selfless worker for the sport; and Wally Holland and Al Murray, long-standing friends and cooperators in weightlifting matters.

Very often I see direct or near direct quotes from my research without acknowledgement being given and I would not like to fall into the same trap. I therefore wish to say that my own personal investigations have been greatly assisted by reading up technical articles in BAWLA's **Coaching Journal** and although I have never corresponded with the gentleman, Pete Tulluto deserves great credit for translating important information from the Soviet Union. **The International Olympic Lifter** is another excellent source of authentic lifting information.

The development of weightlifting

Although the history of lifters and lifting is covered in detail elsewhere it will be useful here to take a backward glance at the development of the two lifts to note the many changes over the years.

Since the earliest days of the sport, getting the biggest possible weight overhead was always one of the best loved feats. The great champions of Germany and Austria in the formative years of weight-lifting were very stocky, often portly, men and they put the weight overhead via a series of movements, muscling or 'mauling' up the body and then jerking it overhead with little movement of the feet. The first part of the lift was anything but a 'clean' movement; it took the more athletic French lifters at the turn of the century to popularise this phase. Prior to this the Germans found that if after the pull, the legs were swiftly bent, the bar could be more easily received at the chest. So the bar was now being put overhead by lifting the weight from the ground to waist level, usually allowing it to rest behind the buckle of the stout belts which they wore. A second pull and a heave from the legs took the bar to the chest, the knees bending a little to catch the bar on the clavicles and deltoids. The final part was of course jerking the bar overhead, and a little step forward was introduced; later some lifters even shuffled their feet, one forwards and the other backwards.

The French lifters, favouring a more agile approach, took the weight clean to the chest in one movement and introduced the split, one foot moving forwards and the other backwards at the same time. The split was used in the jerk as well as the clean. Naturally there was debate

9

and some cross-fertilisation, different styles being used in each country. The general picture which emerged was that in Germany and Austria there was a tradition of what became known as the 'Continental Clean', although the term is in itself a contradiction as the two movements are not 'clean'. When the one movement became statutory these lifters preferred to squat rather than split, whereas the French preferred to clean and favoured the split style.

Britain was much slower off the mark and a review of early instructional books is most revealing. The two-hand snatch was rarely mentioned, although the one-hand variation was more popular. Arthur Saxon in his **Textbook of Weightlifting** protested against any foot movement, saying it disturbed balance, was ungainly and wasted effort, although he confessed that in spite of his protests his brothers stepped back with the right foot during the clean. However, he was advanced in one way; as far back as 1906 in **The Development of Physical Power** he advocated the second pull as part of the clean — 'after raising the bar to a certain height give it another pull just as it is about to commence going down again as you dip beneath it, and this final pull, which is hard to describe, should mean a good 10 lb, or even 15 lb, to you once you have thoroughly mastered it'.

Looking up at the bar was standard practice and taught by most instructors for the first quarter of the new century. Later when Inch began teaching the split clean and split jerk (**The Art and Science of Lifting**) he expressed his preference for a half split/half squat style — what could be called a splat or a squit, for it was neither one nor the other and combined the worst features of each. Inch was also roundly abused for overestimating human possibilities when in the first decade of this century he forecast the following records for the clean and jerk:

112 lb class — 200 lb
119 lb class — 210 lb
126 lb class — 225 lb
140 lb class — 250 lb
160 lb class — 280 lb
Heavies — 350 lb

The 1986 clean and jerk records, rounded up after conversion from kilograms, are:

114 ½ lb class — 336 lb
123 ¼ lb class — 376 lb
132 ¼ lb class — 409 lb
148 ¾ lb class — 441 lb
165 ¼ lb class — 446 lb
220 ¼ lb class — 530 lb
242 ½ lb class — 580 lb

In Attila's book **The Art of Weightlifting and Muscular Development** (1903) the jerk is described as follows:

'The left foot should be placed slightly in front of the right. The elbows must rest on the body. To do this it is necessary to allow the shoulders to droop. In this position the weight is jerked from off the body and as before explained a far greater weight can be raised this way than if the elbows are unsupported. Bend the knees a little and suddenly straighten them; this will shoot the bar up over the head when the left foot must shoot forwards and the right foot backwards simultaneously, which will allow you to place the straightened arms beneath the bar.'

It is worth noting this book also was edited by Thomas Inch.

The First World War over weightlifting soon became worldwide, especially after its introduction to the Olympic Games at Antwerp in 1920. The split style of lifting became most popular, perhaps because of the inspiration and influence of the great French champions, Cadine and Charles Rigoulot. Cadine was the star of the 1920 Olympics and Rigoulot was the first to clean and jerk 400 lb, using an extremely long springy bar instead of standard equipment. There were, however, several other reasons why the squat style was not popular. The split was used for the jerk so such foot movements were practised and accepted by all. In the snatch the rule had prevented hand spacing wider than shoulder width. This resulted in the lifter having to sit very upright and in the squat this was precarious, with the narrow hand spacing allowing little shoulder mobility. Often the lifters would rise on to their toes and the very small base meant many missed lifts. The newest style brought with it a new breed of lifters: split and thin were in and squat and stout were out. In the mid-1930s Egyptian lifters were proving very successful in international competition and people were beginning to copy the styles of Touni, Shams and Fayad. They had a peculiar way of splitting which became known as the camel hop.

The change of popularity from squat to split came gradually, first in the clean and later in the snatch where the narrow hand spacing had long since been discarded, although the Germans, who had many great champions, had always remained faithful to the squat style. It is my view that the big swing towards the squat style was due to American influence in the 1940s and 50s, particularly the example of the 'boy wonder' Pete George, whose prodigious poundages

Saleh of Egypt: the camel hop

Pete George, the best-known and most successful exponent of the dislocation style

and platform personality as a mere youth electrified audiences from all parts of the globe.

Tommy Kono and the splendid Russian lifters showed the fantastic possibilities of sound squatting techniques and gradually the style spread even to the British school, the keenest adherents of the split style, due to the dynamic campaigning of Al Murray, National Coach for twenty years up to 1968. In the immediate post-war era, Al Murray did more than anyone else to put weightlifting coaching on a sound theoretical basis by incorporating anatomy and body mechanics into his teaching. When the squat style did take over there were variations just as there had been in splitting and like the Egyptian camel hop, the Japanese frog kick had its followers. Top lifters like the Miyakes created this fashion.

The Russian entry into international weightlifting gave us a completely new Iron Game. While I spent months in my study doing cine analysis and experimenting in gyms with crude lights on ends of bars to discover paths of movements, the Russians brought in force plates and electronics to accelerate knowledgeable progress and thus moved ahead of the rest of

Dr Arcady Vorobyev, chief of Russia's College of Physical Culture, making a presentation to the author

the world in technical know-how. I was most impressed when I visited the Physical Culture Institute in Moscow (1975) and Dr Arcady Vorobiev gave me a conducted tour explaining the sophisticated apparatus in their laboratories, classrooms and weight rooms.

Apart from my specto-analyser, only on rare occasions had I had access to advanced apparatus at a university, but there in the USSR they had their own very expensive equipment for use by lifters and coaches for every training session.

Lifting techniques

Moving on now to the technical section, I would like to note that I have learned a great deal, first from Jim Mackintosh, Scotland's first Chief Coach and now in charge of physical education at Kentucky University, and Al Murray who has already been mentioned. In turn, I have always tried to pass on the results of my own research and film analysis, and although some of my findings were very controversial at the time, they have now become very widely accepted. The re-bending of the knees (second knee bend) during the pull is probably the best example of this and I am proud to have been the first to publicise this important lifting technique. The crucial factor in my research is the study of the best lifters in the world doing their maximum attempts in competitions. This eliminated the shortcomings of some otherwise interesting studies. The following sections will outline the most effective techniques and training methods and while I will delve deeply into the principles and key factors, I will try to avoid an academic approach and emphasise practical advice which will improve performances.

The width of the grip and the type of hold are important first considerations. The width of the grip is affected by several factors including the relative strength of the muscles in the pull and overhead, the mobility of the shoulders and the lifter's physical characteristics such as the breadth of his shoulders. In the snatch the hands should be at least 'elbow wide' — by that I mean the distance between the elbows when the upper arms are held horizontally in line with the shoulders. This is approximately 750cm (30in) in a man of average physique. If the lifter lacks shoulder mobility or he has difficulty in keeping his trunk upright in the low position of the snatch, then the hands should take a wider grip.

In the clean and jerk the hands should normally be at approximately shoulder width, those having tight shoulders taking a slightly wider grasp. It should be remembered that there is a loss of pulling power with a wider grip so compromise or change in grip is necessary. In the old days when taking hold of the bar, lifters would often have their thumbs on the same side of the bar as their fingers, probably a hang-over from thick shafted dumb-bells. The 'thumbs around' grip became standard and then the 'hook grip' took over the clean and later on the snatch as records became heavier. It is this hook grip which is recommended here. The grip is one of the weakest links in the chain so special methods must be adopted and in the hook, the thumb is first placed around the bar and then the first, and sometimes the second finger, are positioned **over** the thumb to lock it on the bar.

Make sure you know the measurement of your grip on the bar and if you find yourself training or competing on a barbell to which you are

unaccustomed use a tape for accuracy in measuring the correct hand spacing. On standard bars it is customary to use your fingers to measure out the position of the hands.

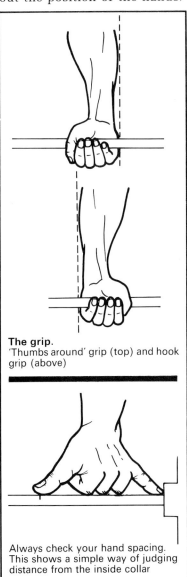

The grip.
'Thumbs around' grip (top) and hook grip (above)

Always check your hand spacing. This shows a simple way of judging distance from the inside collar

15

The starting position

In Britain and Japan over the years, there has been a marked tendency to start the lift with heels together but personally I have always advised a foot spacing equivalent to hip width. Most of the champions of the Soviet Union have used this technique with obvious exceptions such as Alexeev. A narrow spacing would be with feet 150 to 250cm (6 to 10in) apart, medium 250 to 350cm (10 to 14in) and wide 350 to 450cm (14 to 18in) but obviously the size of the lifter's feet has a bearing on this matter.

The bar should be over the instep, not over the toes.

Back and leg positions

The back is kept flat (but not horizontal or vertical) and the legs are well bent, arms straight, knuckles to the front, and shoulders over the bar. My research shows that in the snatch most champions have their backs at an angle of between 16° and 25° and most of these are in the lower end of the range. In the clean, however, the back was much steeper because of the narrower hand spacing which meant the shoulders rose

higher. In both snatch and clean the thighs are above horizontal as the bar comes off the platform.

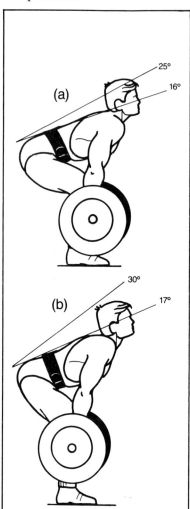

Snatch technique.
(a) As the bar comes off the platform the back is at an angle of between 16° and 25° to the horizontal
(b) The bar is about to pass the knees. The back is now at an angle of between 17° and 30°: most of the work has been done by the legs

Key positions during the lift

There are a number of key positions in a lift and faults will quickly be spotted if checked against correct placing of the body as it passes through these key areas. The widely accepted key positions are:

As the bar leaves the platform

As the bar passes the knees

The position of full extension of the body

The highest point of the pull before the bar starts to drop

The lowest position in the snatch or clean

In the jerk the key positions are:

The starting position, bar held at the chest

At the lowest point of the dip

At the highest point of the drive before the feet split

The lowest position in the split

Louis Martin in the lowest position of the snatch

I would add one other position and that is during the second part of the pull where the knees should be pushed forward prior to this so-called second pull.

The first pull, taking the bar to and past the knees

In the first part of the pull you must aim at raising the head and hips at the same rate. In modern lifting, largely because of the influence of the Bulgarians, there is an effort to lift the bar quickly and build up acceleration during this phase. In overcoming the inertia of the bar there is a danger of the hips coming up much faster than the head, which reduces angular momentum, i.e. there is a slowing down on the trunk rotating around the hip joint. You must therefore guard against the back rounding and the shoulders coming up slower than the hips, thus losing the starting angle of the back. The first fast thrust must come from the massive muscles of the thigh and the hip muscle action on the femur, and the starting angle of the back must be retained.

As the bar is taken from the floor to pass the knees it should travel slightly backwards over the centre of the foot. The legs straighten to

allow the backward travel of the bar to take place.

The bar and body should be kept as close as possible throughout the pull.

The bar should deviate slightly from a straight line of travel; this trajectory will be described as we go on. Suffice it to say at this stage that if the shoulders go back too soon the bar will travel backwards. The shoulders **should** move forward, a characteristic apparent in all the great champions with the heavier weights having shoulders further forward than lighter men. The arms should incline from the vertical to an angle of approximately 20°. If the barbell is incorrectly taken backwards the shoulders will not move as far forward — the shoulders vertically over the position is usually a sign that the bar is being pulled slightly too far backwards.

I see many slight changes in technique and lifting fashions over the years and whereas it was common only a few years ago for the legs to be very nearly straight as the bar passed the knees, an angle of 170° to 180° seems more common now.

Miyake of Japan during the first pull (left) and after the second knee bend, with arms still straight. A strong position

The second knee bend

As the bar passes the knees the legs should be almost straight and shoulders still forward. Speed of bar and body acceleration will have built up and a significant change takes place. The knees are re-bent to put the knees under the bar and the thighs and bar as close together as possible. It is important that the knees go forward rather than the bar be pulled back to any great extent. Pushing the knees forward under the bar produces a re-bending of the knees, puts the hips forward and makes the the hips drop slightly, but the benefits of the improved position more than compensate for this slight lowering of the pelvis. Lifters who have practised this technique can get their knees 100-150cm (4 to 6in) further forward than those who do not make a conscious effort to get their knees under the bar. A number of good lifters unconsciously use this knee action, indicating that it comes naturally to those with good kinaesthetic sense. Placing the hamstring muscles on stretch as the bar passes the knees helps create a stretch reflex which will, if properly channelled, result in the knee position advocated.

The knees under the bar position described is a very strong one from which to pull

Talts of the USSR. Pushing forward the knees can give great leg thrust at the top of the pull

hard to complete this all-important phase of the lift. Mechanical and anatomical factors are all very favourable for an explosive pull which will make the bar travel upwards as the lifter goes under it into a low position. The legs and back, working in their inner range, are capable of exerting great power in this position; the calves can add momentum to the bar as they cause the body to rise on the toes. There is a further muscle group which should be brought into action at the top of the pull and that is the muscles of the shoulder girdle, particularly the trapezius which, lifting the shoulders, can add further momentum and height to the bar.

The arms bend, left late in the pull, has the double effect of taking the bar higher and pulling the body under the bar at the same time. If the arms bend too much, too early, they do not help pull the body into a good position.

When in the knees under the bar position, the arms are almost vertical, with very little flexion. The forward and upward thrust of the hips should not be overlooked in bringing the body to extension, but I believe this has become a rather outdated technique and the second knee bend with powerful **upward** and slightly forward thrust is very much the modern style.

Finishing the pull

The last part of the pull is important not only because of the strength which can be utilised but also because it is the part of the lift which has the greatest effect on the direction and momentum of the bar at the most crucial stage, as the lift is completed.

At the top of the pull the bar should be travelling as nearly as possible straight upwards. The bar usually travels a little forward here but if it goes too far the lifter will have no chance of holding the weight in a low position. On the other hand, if the bar starts travelling backwards at this stage, you have no chance of successfully completing the lift as there is a 'hook' putting even more backward movement on the bar as the lifter goes under the weight. If the shoulders move back too early or the hips go too far back then the bar will move back.

The full extension

The arms do not play a major role until the body is almost fully extended. The arms should be kept straight as long as possible — beginners in particular tend to use the arms much too soon. The extensors of the hip are much more important in the final drive than the arms but they too

21

must be correctly used, pushing the body into an upright position instead of leaning backwards. The angle of the legs greatly affects the direction in which the bar will travel.

In getting to the position of full extension, it is important to apply **maximum force** for the **maximum distance and time**. That means pulling as **fast** as possible for as long as possible, and this also means pulling yourself under the bar. Incidentally, it is no use completely extending after the feet have left the floor — power comes from the ground.

The next point links the fully extended position and the following stage. I have stressed that arms should be kept fairly straight during the pull — just out of the locked position is fine. I have also pointed out that many lifters bend their arms too much and too soon. This brings the bar much higher than it need be to allow the lifter to get under it. The coach who trains his lifters to pull the bar high is doing them a disservice. He should be channelling their energies into acquiring the ability to get under the bar, pulled to only a low position.

At first sight, this may seem a strange assertion, so we must examine it in detail. First, you should be aware that because of the different widths of hand spacing the pull for the snatch will be higher than it is for the clean. You can check this by standing in the upright position with a shoulder width grip and then moving your hands to a wide snatch width grip; you will see that the bar height is raised.

In my cine-analysis I have been struck by the fact that many of the most athletic record holders, particularly in the lighter classes, can get under the weight successfully although they do not pull very high. Other much stronger and heavier men find it necessary to pull the bar higher to get under it before it drops. In my earlier book **The Development of the Clean and Jerk** I compiled tables of those who pulled the bar to above standing belt height, i.e. the height of the lifting belt while the lifter was in the upright position, and I pointed out that if the heavies could employ the same techniques as the lighter men then the records would be much higher. The heavies sometimes pull as much as 15 per cent higher and that to me seems a lot of wasted potential. Just imagine how much heavier weights they could lift to crutch height instead of belt height.

Cultivate the speed, power and body positions to get under the bar, fast and low, although it has not been pulled to standing belt height. People

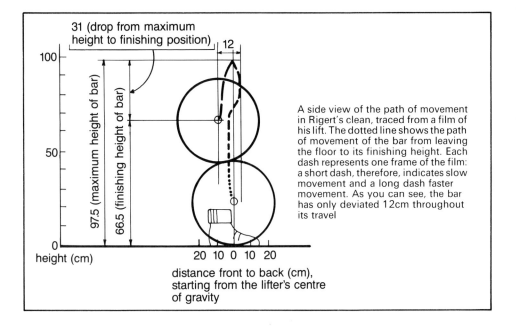

31 (drop from maximum height to finishing position) ‖ 12

100

97.5 (maximum height of bar)

66.5 (finishing height of bar)

50

0

height (cm)

20 10 0 10 20

distance front to back (cm), starting from the lifter's centre of gravity

A side view of the path of movement in Rigert's clean, traced from a film of his lift. The dotted line shows the path of movement of the bar from leaving the floor to its finishing height. Each dash represents one frame of the film: a short dash, therefore, indicates slow movement and a long dash faster movement. As you can see, the bar has only deviated 12cm throughout its travel

tended to scoff when I said that the 250kg clean was not far away if a super heavy could use this technique and I was proved right. Research has shown that the splitters for the snatch and the clean invariably pull the bar higher than squatters before they begin to go under the weight: yet another reason why the squat style is more effective for most people.

While on this point let me say that some of the so-called assistance exercises for the pull actually aggravate the bent-arm fault rather than cure it. All assistance work should be aimed at improving the good points of technique, not perfecting mistakes, as is so often the case.

To turn to the anatomical aspects of the movement, the order in which muscles are brought into play is of prime importance. To overcome the inertia of the bar in the starting position the big, strong, heavy muscles are brought into play. These are situated near your centre of gravity with the hips as the centre point and the back and thighs on either side. As the movement progresses momentum is gained. The somewhat weaker, lighter but faster muscles are added on and it will be observed that the sequence of muscle action is one which flows from the centre of the body outwards. After the hips, thighs and back come the trapezius, deltoids,

23

arm flexors and wrist extensors in that order; in the lower body the ankle extensors are the last to be brought into play. In this way the muscles are utilised to produce maximum efficiency with acceleration, which will give you the correct **timing** for the lift.

It goes without saying that there is a slight overlapping of muscle action otherwise the input of one group would be expended before the next took over. This overlap gives the smooth but fast acceleration which is the hallmark of the expert.

The 'second pull', as some people call the next part of the action, is really a misnomer. There is no sign of its producing any further acceleration of the bar and rather than teach lifters this arm pull, I prefer to teach the proper sequence of movement with the arm action delayed until the lifter is ready to go under the bar, when it can be coordinated with the maximum effort of legs and back.

Over the years I have advised a forward and upward hip thrust as the legs are extended and here I will describe the positions which I hope will be achieved by this type of hip thrust. The aim, of course, is the full extension of the body, and a vigorous hip thrust will make this possible. However, the body can be fully extended — even hyper-extended — and still be in a bad position.

You can best appreciate this by looking at the illustrations of the 'line of thrust'. This is a line drawn from the hip joint to the centre of the base when in the position of maximum extension during any given lift. This shows the direction of the thrust being applied by the lifter in that lift. For example, if

The line of thrust.
The lifter on the right, whilst demonstrating a very efficient line of thrust, is in a position seldom if ever achieved in reality. A good one to aim for, though!
(Right) the line of thrust is perpendicular and the hips are forward of the shoulders. (Left) the line of thrust is backwards and the shoulders are forwards of the hips — a very inefficient position

the hips are back and the body not fully extended, the lifter will almost certainly move back as he goes under the bar. If the lifter extends fully but has not used the forward and upward hip thrust his hips will still be behind the base and therefore he will again move backwards. Another fairly common fault is to put the hips forward but use a faster more dynamic head and shoulder action which rotates the upper body backwards. Again, because the overall tendency of the extension is backwards, the lifter is likely to jump back. The best position will show the body fully extended and hips well forward over the feet. The more upright the legs, the more this will direct the bar upwards and the better the chance of getting directly under the weight. The full extension of the body including the trunk, is extremely important and a small amount of backward lean (approximately 7° to 14°) can be expected at the end of the pull.

Getting under the bar

In modern lifting, getting under the bar usually means dropping into a squat rather than a split, but both styles will be covered. As well as pulling hard with the arms, the lifter must thrust the hips down and forward under the bar. It is not enough to simply drop downwards — there must be thrust and drive, getting low as quickly as possible. The feet should be off the floor for the minimum length of time.

The actions involved at the top of the pull and in getting under the bar puts a little hook on to the trajectory of the bar and the end result is largely pre-determined by this; the smaller the hook (i.e. the less displacement there is to the bar) the easier it will be to reach a correct balanced low position. A big hook will mean the bar is travelling backwards; experienced lifters will know how difficult it is to hold a bar which is travelling backwards at this point. The correct finish to your pull will help eliminate this fault — that is why leg and trunk position in the pull is so important. Many coaches also stress that the elbows should be sideways as the arms bend, rather than backwards, as backwards pointing elbows often lead to backward pulls.

Lifters who have hooking problems should check on their hand and wrist action at this stage of the lift. The bar is heavier and less mobile than the body, and you are aiming at minimal bar displacement, so the hands and arms should rotate round the axis of the bar rather than the hands flicking/

How to avoid hooking problems. When lowering the body in the snatch, rotate the hands and arms around the axis of the bar

hooking the bar backwards.

The pulling up of the legs by the lifter as he 'dives' under the bar has long been taught by successful Eastern bloc coaches. Obviously there is a need for some 'braking' after this, as the lifter sinks to the lowest position. The feet should move to slightly more than shoulder width apart and turn out to 20° to 25°. If the feet are turned out more than this, the size of the base (on a forward/backward plane) will be reduced and this is most detrimental. If the feet go wider apart it will be hard to rise with the weights. Aim to have the

feet land in line with the starting position but take into account that with maximum weights the feet may move back a trifle as you go into the squat. Significant backward movement of the feet indicates an inefficient backward pull

In the most effective low position the feet move apart a little without moving backwards and the lifter gets his hips as close as possible to his heels, the knees going forward and sideways pointing in the same direction as his toes. Squatting in a low position like this allows the lifter to sit fairly upright. The upper back and arms must be quite vertical. **This is in complete contrast to the dislocation styles widely taught in America not so long ago.** The theory there was that with the high bottom position the hips should be raised and the head lowered if the bar had a tendency to drop back. 'To counter the weight when caught too far forward, the hips may be lowered and the head raised'. This technique is not recommended. The low hip, vertical arm position is the one I prefer.

There is a school of thought which advocates going down only as low as necessary, i.e. if the weight is light you do not need to go so low, while with heavy weights you will be forced into a low position. I do not subscribe to this view. The lifter must go down **faster** than

Julian Creus of Great Britain going under the bar in the less effective split style

the bar in order that he can be in the correct position to receive it. The way to do this is to keep pulling with the arms and make a conscious effort to get your legs moving into the receiving position. To emphasise the different character of the pull and the drop under the weight, I used to advise my lifters to 'pull like a strong man and drop like a ballet dancer'. Alas, too many pull like ballet dancers and drop like strong men.

The camel hop and high-jumping styles of the past are out-moded now for the simple reason that **power comes from the ground.** It is the pressure exerted on the ground which gives you the drive and getting

Alan Winterbourne. The unsupported phase: Alan pulls himself quickly under the bar in the more efficient squat style

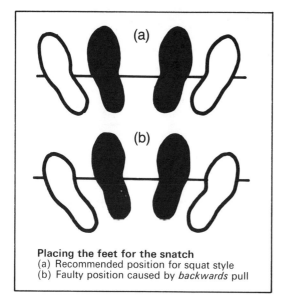

Placing the feet for the snatch
(a) Recommended position for squat style
(b) Faulty position caused by *backwards* pull

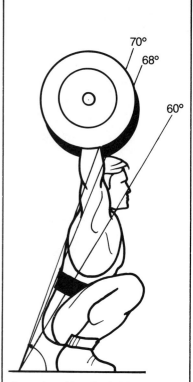

A good position, back fairly upright. The 68° angle illustrated is the sort of position lifters with normal mobility can attain. The 60° angle would indicate a dislocation style. 70° shows above average mobility

the feet back on the ground quickly after the split or squat gives you the control you need. Once again the squat cleaner has the advantage over the splitter as he has less distance to move his feet. This poses the question 'Why move the feet at all?', which throws up the possibilities of interesting compromises to evolve a new technique, but the answer is that first the feet must be placed to allow maximum leg drive then changed to the best position in which to successfully receive the bar while in the low position. That is not the end of the story, the feet must be in the right position to produce a good recovery and bring the body upright — and this is particularly important in the heaviest cleans where every bit of leg strength is necessary. When Louis Martin was encountering problems in rising with maximum poundages, to try to improve the situation measurements were taken of feet spacings in scores of his snatches, cleans and squats. As a result of this, modifications of technique were made to give him better foot spacings for his recovery,

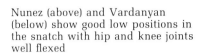

which worked well. He
eventually cleaned and
recovered with more than he
could jerk.

Recovering with the weight

In the snatch the recovery
presents no difficulties for
splitters and little difficulty for
squatters unless they have
very tight shoulders. Splitters
are advised to recover by
extending the legs and
thrusting on the front leg to
move the foot back and then
bringing the rear foot forwards
to place the feet in line for the
referee's signal.

In squat snatching, the
weight must be kept settled
back safely to prevent it going
forwards and out of control as
the hips are raised; it is for this
reason that good shoulder
mobility is essential. Avoid
raising the hips much faster
than the shoulders otherwise
you will find a tendency to
'dislocate' by rotation of the
shoulder which will cause you
to lose the weight backwards.

In both styles the recovery
should be affected without
delay. As soon as the weight is
correctly received the legs are
straightened, taking advantage
of any rebound.

29

In the clean it must be admitted that the splitters have (or had) an easier time in the recovery phase. Very seldom have splitters failed to stand up with a weight they have pulled in. The favourable mechanics allow the splitter to overcome inertia by pushing on the front foot in a backward and upward direction. With the weight moving upwards towards the centre of a very wide front-to-back base the back leg acts as a pivot and lever, making the front foot recovery comparatively simple. This is followed by a small step forward as described for the snatch.

In the squat clean the situation is very different. The weight is often pulled in very well but the lifter cannot stand up with it, being unable to straighten his legs. The 'sticking point' is well known and all sorts of manoeuvres are used to combat this.

First let me say that you must at all costs avoid stopping at the sticking point, for once the weight stops its upward journey, failure is almost certain. Bouncing several times, as some lifters do, to gain momentum, is very hard on knee joints but catching the weight on the bounce and profiting by the rebound of thigh on calf is a legitimate and valid device

Andrew Davies gets his elbow forward and up in the clean

which can and should be used.

Many lifters who settle in the low position begin their recovery by tipping the hips backwards and upwards and then drive strongly with the legs. Those who employ this style must be very careful that they keep the elbows well up or else the weight will be lost forward.

Yet another method is to drive strongly upwards and as the hardest point is reached the hips are tipped backwards with little, if any, forward displacement of the bar. This device increases the angle between the bones of the upper leg and those of the lower leg thus overcoming the infamous sticking point. Having done this, however, the lifter must re-adjust his balance forcing head and shoulders upwards and hips forward and upwards.

While some shifting of balance is permissible, and often advantageous in the recovery, excessive rounding of the back or other unorthodox movements will bring a danger of injury.

It is not unusual to see lifters trying to get through the sticking point by forcing their knees inwards at the crucial stage but this is extremely wearing on the knee joints and should be discouraged. I much prefer a straightforward 'power' recovery and advise lifters to practise front squats using exactly the same foot spacing and hand positions as they do in the clean, duplicating the position as closely as possible. However, if adjustments have to be made, these should be **kept to the minimum and re-adjustment made as quickly as possible.** Obviously, economy of effort in the recovery is of prime importance because the lift is far from finished. It must still be jerked overhead and a difficult clean is psychologically bad. Aim at easy cleans and good recoveries but train yourself to accept difficulties in the early stages. You should be confident that if you can get the weight to the chest you will be able to ram it overhead in good style.

As you reach the final upright position make sure you have the bar in a good position from which to jerk from the shoulders.

We have now covered the all-important pulling techniques for the snatch and for the clean, considering the split style and the squat style. The recovery in the snatch and the clean have also been reviewed and now our attention is turned to the second part of the clean and jerk — the jerk itself. In this we will ignore variations of no-split and half-split techniques which have from time to time appeared on the scene. These have little significance in a book aimed at showing the way to maximum performance. We will deal only with the orthodox split technique which is the best and quickest way to success.

The jerk

In describing the pull for snatching and cleaning we began with the grip on the bar, and we must do the same for the jerk.

Although the hook grip is advised during the pull it is certainly not advised for the jerk. It would actually be a disadvantage, so the hook must be released. Many lifters actually release the hook during the recovery from the clean, a time when the wrists are often very much extended; the weight may even come on to the fingertips. I know several lifters whose little fingers come off the bar. These lifters would be well advised to note my comments about getting the weight into a good jerking position as they thrust upwards at the **final** part of the recovery.

However, it is also true to say that many champion lifters

The brilliant David Morgan of Great Britain shows a solid, balanced position in the clean

actually adjust their grip round the bar during the early part of the jerk. The noted Plyukfelder (USSR) was quite astounding to watch as he would completely re-grip the bar at this stage; he would also mess about in training by actually taking the dip with one hand spacing and during the jerk would widen this spacing considerably! This was just one of Rudy Plyukfelder's many lifting idiosyncrasies — a most interesting lifter. The one thing I would stress about the grip prior to jerking is that there is no need to grip the bar hard — a very loose grasp is quite acceptable and preferable to setting up tensions which have a cumulative effect on other factors involved in the lift.

While lifters must not hold the weight at the shoulders for a long time, it is important that they settle the bar and themselves correctly. The calming effect is a necessary part of the lift and research has shown that a hurried jerk, not pausing sufficiently at the shoulders, was a significant source of failures in the lift. The pause must be long enough for the lifter to be comfortably positioned, poised and composed for a maximum, controlled effort. It should be no longer than this for waiting too long before jerking is just as bad (although not as common) as being too hurried.

Morgan (above) and Blagoev of Bulgaria (overleaf): wide splitting, powerful jerks

The same kinetic principles for the snatch and the clean are applied in the jerk but in a different way. The feet should be parallel with each other and placed hip width apart. The knee bend (dip for the jerk) is the movement used so that the big strong muscles around the centre of gravity can be brought into play. These are used first and the shoulders, arms and calves are used later in the thrust. Some lifters use too much arm strength too soon in the belief that it gives better direction and control.

You can generally identify these lifters by their low elbow positions. We can learn a lot from a review of out-dated styles and I would point to the fact that even in the now defunct press, arm power became less important than the thrust from the hips and back (and even loosely locked legs!). The fast pressers too had their elbows well forward. One other point to consider — too early and too much arm action will upset the timing of the lift. Keep to the policy of using big strong muscles first and the small weaker ones later.

In the dip for the jerk direction is all important. Aim at going directly down and directly back up with the minimum of bar displacement. The feet should be kept flat on the floor during this dip. There has been only one exception to this rule — Huska of Hungary — among all the world champions I have studied.

The necessary dip is often underestimated and a number of good lifters would profit by a bigger and more speedy dip and thrust. One of the most significant pieces of lifting research from the Orient shows that a significant number of jerks fail not so much because of lack of strength on the part of the lifter, but because of failings in technique, e.g. insufficient knee bend in the dip.

The researcher Chu Tse-

Vardanyan's narrow foot spacing means his rear leg bends more, and although he hollows his back he still has a strong arm movement

35

Phil Grippaldi of the USA (above); the bar is directly over his head and his arms are straight. (Opposite): Bar and body are out of alignment

Chiao stated that the two main causes of failure were starting the jerk too early and not enough knee bend in the dip (although there are of course other very common reasons for failure at a later stage of the lift). Chu Tse-Chiao suggested that the knees be bent to 110° to 115°; British researchers, looking at general athletic performance rather than at weightlifting specifically, have found that 115° between calves and thighs allows the most vigorous extension of the thigh.

My own measurements and observations show that the champions bend to a maximum of 110° and the least bend is around 120°. These independent investigations support the recommendation of 110° to 115° bend.

There is a lot of misunderstanding concerning the thrust prior to the jerk. Just as in the pull, force must be applied over as long a distance as possible but what is not normally given much thought is that without a decent dip the thrust would be a very short one indeed. Let me elaborate.

In a good thrust, about 60 per cent would be as a result of the dip and the remaining 40 per cent — before the feet leave the ground — would be the difference between normal standing height and the full extension caused by rising on the toes prior to the split.

It would be detrimental to alter these proportions by (a) reducing the depth of dip or (b) increasing the thrust by using more arm strength prior to the split. The soundest technique is to split as a flowing continuation of the thrust, with the feet moving as soon as the legs can no longer add further momentum to the bar.

A remarkable number of otherwise knowledgeable lifters have no idea how short the thrust really is. In the majority of cases, and I am referring to champions, the

split begins when the thrust has just lifted the bar off the chest and is no more than throat or chin level. This will be a revelation to most lifters, I am certain.

Once again speed is all important. In the very short time between the feet leaving the ground — when the bar is no higher than chin level — and the time that the feet land **the arms must almost straighten.** A very strong arm movement is, of course, essential and this has a two-way effect. It helps get the body under the bar **and** transfers momentum to the bar as soon as the feet land.

In splitting, the feet **should** always leave the ground at precisely the same instant whether in the snatch, the

37

clean or the jerk, but unfortunately, it is very seldom this happens. Instead, lifters nearly always **anticipate** the split and before the extension is concluded they automatically begin transferring their weight (on to what becomes the forward foot) so that they can easily take away the foot which goes backwards. This has a very detrimental effect. Firstly, it robs the lifter of a **two-legged thrust.** Secondly, it gives one leg more work than the other and thirdly, it upsets balance because the barbell also begins to move to one side as the weight is transferred. This fault is very common indeed and some lifters anticipate so much that even in the dip they begin shifting their body weight on to one leg.

When split snatching was in vogue, 'pulling on one leg', as we call this, was the most common fault of all. When you see a lifter stagger sideways with a weight, take note of the direction in which he initially staggers. Almost always it will be to the same side as his forward leg. This is because the weight will have started in this direction when there was a transfer of weight prior to splitting. The correction of the fault lies in concentration on a good dip with weight equally balanced on both feet (your coach or training mate should watch from the rear and will easily spot any favouring of one leg) and a good drive with **both** legs before the feet leave the floor. It is almost impossible to get both feet moving off the ground at exactly the same time and the experiments I have done on force plates show that it is in any case not absolutely crucial that they do. I often found that although the back foot moved faster and further, the front foot was virtually unweighted at the same time so there was no loss of balance with the best lifters. If there is any sign of poor balance check on this point at once. If one end of the bar is lower than the other during the jerk or one arm appears to straighten first, check again for weight transference as these are symptoms of this fault.

Arm action in the jerk

Recapping on the starting position for the jerk, the elbows should be raised so that the weight is carried not by the arms but by the shoulders. The drive from the legs is transmitted to the bar and the weight will rise to around throat or chin height before the feet leave the ground. The dynamic thrust will carry the bar upwards so that as the feet land the arms will almost be straight. The **slight** bending of the legs will 'cushion' the heavy weight and will lower the body enough to allow the arms to straighten. However, the legs must be firm enough to give a good base for the very strong arm action which must be used at the conclusion of the jerk. It should go without saying that maximum arm strength is used in conjunction with the other muscle groups.

The lifter must avoid three things which will make arm action very difficult in the final lock out:

1 **bringing the triceps into play too soon or other movements which put the bar out in front**
2 **moving back from the weight so that the shoulders are behind the hands at the completion of the jerk, and**
3 **failing to follow through vigorously, getting shoulders and head under the bar at the end of the jerk.**

Let us look at these points in more detail.

I teach what I have termed the 'open' jerk, for in this the elbows are consciously opened as the lift is performed. It is not unnatural for the elbows to move from their forward position into their final overhead position in a direct straight line. However, I prefer to whip the elbows **sideways as soon as the bar is in flight** so that they are **under** the bar as quickly as possible. In the former method they are not

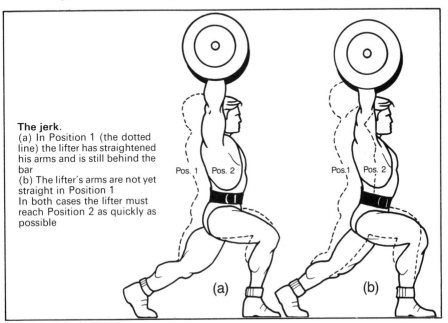

The jerk.
(a) In Position 1 (the dotted line) the lifter has straightened his arms and is still behind the bar
(b) The lifter's arms are not yet straight in Position 1
In both cases the lifter must reach Position 2 as quickly as possible

Pos. 1 Pos. 2 (a)

Pos.1 Pos. 2 (b)

under the bar until the arms are finally locked and this is not only mechanically less efficient, there is always the tendency for the shoulders to keep back when this style is used.

The next factor spotlights another of the most common faults when there are failures in the jerk. How many times do you see a lifter get the weight to arms' length or nearly to arms' length overhead, and simply fail to hold it? It is a common sight and while failing with a weight that is too heavy for the lifter is excusable, there is no excuse whatsoever for many of the failures — they are due to poor technique. Yet I have heard lifters in such circumstances ask for advice and be given wrong information. 'You put the bar out in front' is the normal explanation given and while this is sometimes the case, I have seen many instances when the bar was in the right place and the lifter was too far back from the bar — which is entirely different.

Two positions are illustrated:
a **When the lifter has straightened the arms but is still behind the weight; and**
b **the more common landing position, when the feet hit the floor and the arms are still slightly bent.**

In both cases there must be a decided effort to get the head and shoulders under the bar in time with a slight sinking of the body, by thrusting the front knee forward. All too often there is the sink without the head and shoulder action. A very positive attitude is required in this movement and if you can master this combination, then success in jerking will be yours.

On a coaching note, you can always tell if a lifter has put the bar forward or the lifter has stayed behind the bar, by comparing the starting and finishing positions of the bar. The observant coach will always locate the bar position in relation to static objects in the background. It becomes second nature after a time and it is a practice worth cultivating, for body position alone tells only part of the story.

The path of the bar in jerking

The dip brings the bar very slightly forward as the knees and hips are flexed. The jerk proper puts the bar on an almost vertical path. At the end of the lift there is a slight movement backwards. If there is undue movement backwards (amounting to more than 3in to 4in) the lift is likely to be lost. The more vertical the path of movement in the jerk, the better the lift. In recovering

Milser of West Germany: his excellent technique is a result of good coaching

from the split, once again the front foot is moved back slightly and the rear foot is brought up into line. Be meticulous in this as even champions have been disqualified for their feet being out of position; there is the classic case of John Bolton of New Zealand who lost a Gold Medal at the Commonwealth Games because of this fault. These then are the basic techniques of the snatch and the clean and the jerk. Although there is more written here than in almost all other books on the classic lifts, I assure you I have only scratched the surface and there is a great deal more to learn, particularly on the theoretical side, so that you can understand the cause and effects of various movements and idiosyncrasies. The more knowledge you acquire the better will be your lifting, your coaching, and your appreciation and enjoyment of lifting.

Learning sequence

For the sake of clarity I have broken down the lifts into various sections or phases but it must be remembered that the actions and positions described are very inter-dependent and an inter-relationship exists from start to finish. Having stressed that point, I now feel safe to say that scientific research in the Soviet Union has shown that good lifting technique can be acquired by novices much more quickly if the lift is broken down and taught in sections just as I have done here. However, there is one vital difference. Druzhinin explained that the order of teaching the skills is of paramount importance and strange as it may seem the most effective method of teaching is to do so in reverse order. Ignoring such matters as finding the correct width of grip, etc., the snatch movements were taught thus:

1 The supportive phase of the drop under the bar and standing up (i.e. from the time the feet land on the floor and the recovery). This is taught by the subjects holding a barbell overhead (approx 50 per cent body weight) bringing the arms backwards while inclining the trunk slightly forward and from there dropping as rapidly as possible to the lowest squat position. The same is then done with loss of balance forward and backward so that foot positions can be adjusted.

2 Teaching the non supportive phase going under the bar (i.e. when the body is 'in-flight' the feet having left the floor and not yet landed).
   The exercise recommended is started by standing on the

Sequence photos are a good visual aid when teaching or learning the lift

toes, arms bent at the elbow at an angle of 120°, barbell at abdomen level. The barbell is then raised slowly, torso dropped, feet taken off the floor and the body dropped under the bar into the lowest possible position before the feet touch the floor. The same movement is performed with balance deliberately lost forward and backward so that faults can be automatically corrected.

3 The full extension (what the Soviet coaches call 'preparation for drop under bar').

   Exercise: Stand on toes, bar on upper third of thigh, arms bent to an angle of 150°. Lift the bar, touching thighs and lower abdomen and with slow upward movement, fully extend and drop into the low squat. The same move is then performed with loss of balance forward and backward. Re-position the feet as necessary.

4 Teaching the final pull. (The Russians use the term 'third' pull.) The lift to the knees being first, the second knee bend is the second pull and this final part the third pull. It is taught by having the bar at the level of the lower third of the thigh, heels raised about a centimetre, arms straight at the elbows, and when these positions have been adopted the snatch is done slightly touching the thigh and the lower abdomen and going right through to the finish. As before, there is practice of the same lift, but out of balance.

5 Bringing the knees under the bar (the second knee bend). The bar is at knee level, with shins vertical, arms straight, shoulders in front of bar, all weight resting on the heels. The bar is lifted, moving the knees forward and lightly touching the bar as described in the earlier movements.

6 Lifting to knee level. The bar is taken from the floor, emphasising the first pressure on the toes, moving it rearward with shoulders forward, bringing the bar to the knees and continuing as before.

There you have the inside story of how the coaches of the Soviet Union teach beginners how to snatch. It matches up with widely accepted teaching theory, and remember, this method was devised after considerable experimentation with different sequences of teaching the various movements.

Planning and monitoring a training programme

How to construct a training plan

Many people making up schedules merely string together a few exercises without giving much thought to the character of the various movements or any thought whatever to the order of the exercises. This of course is entirely wrong. Certain points **must** be observed if the schedule is to give maximum benefits and also to be as 'acceptable' as possible. I almost used the word 'enjoyable' in place of 'acceptable', but I had better not say too much about that or I may put off some novices with world championship aspirations! A schedule should be enjoyable, particularly at the elementary stages, and certain things can help in this respect. Remember, though, that the principles outlined here are intended to give best results in every possible way.

The first thing is that all parts of the body should be worked. Avoid missing out squats, for example, because you are not keen on leg work. Even at the very top level, the champions insist that all-round work is included in their schedules.

Secondly, unless there are physical deficiencies, it is undesirable to over-emphasise one particular muscle group. This is not only because such specialisation often causes lop-sided development or unbalanced strength, but it does sometimes destroy techniques, particularly in those with little experience. There is an old saying that 'Strength is the ally of the experienced but the enemy of the novice.' In other words, the novice sometimes uses strength instead of technique and gets into bad lifting habits, and I have noticed that where a man is strong in one direction, he tends to use this strength to the exclusion of other parts which have a good contribution to make.

A gradual 'curve of effort' should be observed in arranging the order of the exercises. The movements should be listed so that during the workout, they become progressively harder in intensity until a peak is reached approximately two-thirds of the way through the schedule, and after these harder exercises, there is a gradual tapering off. Let us elaborate on this a little.

You must start easy in order to limber up, get the blood coursing through the veins, increasing efficiency and decreasing the danger of injury. Only fools take the advice which I have seen given in magazines, to go into the gym and do the hardest exercise first to get them out of the way while you are still fresh. What absolute rubbish! Some physiologists maintain that warming up is not necessary and they say this is only a psychological desire. This just is not true. Perhaps some people do too much warming up, but I defy anybody to do top lifts without loosening up, and furthermore, I wish somebody had told **my** muscles

that warming up was unnecessary; my most severe injuries occurred when I had neglected this aspect of training through various unforeseen circumstances.

In practice, this 'curve of effort' works out well. First there should be a few mobilising exercises, getting the joints working freely and gently stretching the muscles to their maximum so that there are no inhibitions and the minimum of unwanted reflex actions when the real hard work begins. Next you have the lighter resistance exercises, then the hardest ones and finally, the least important ones which are done when your energy may be at a lower ebb. What could be more logical?

One rather fine point: technique work must be done before tiredness sets in. When there is fatigue, the skill element is one of the first to suffer.

There is one last major factor in compiling schedules and this concerns the primary and secondary effects of the exercises. In most exercises more than one group of muscles is worked. The main aim of the exercise we call the primary effect and the second group of muscles is involved in what we call the secondary effect. For example, it may at first appear in order to do a curl for the arm flexors, rowing motion for the latissimus muscles, and then upright rowing exercise for the shoulders. Closer scrutiny, however, reveals that all three work the arm flexors and so the secondary effects of the three consecutive exercises clash, and if three sets of each were done, then there would have been nine sets all working this same muscle group. This does not mean to say that secondary effects must never be the same in the schedule but does suggest that secondary effects and more important primary effects should not clash in consecutive exercises.

You should try to strike a balance in the **type** of exercise. There should be some fast, dynamic movements as well as the slow grinding type of work. Different pieces of apparatus, such as racks, benches and blocks, may be introduced for effect and variety.

Work on a long term plan — that is the aim of this work — so you can see exactly where you are going and what is ahead. When you are a beginner there are so many exercises which are new to you and most of these will do a lot of good. As you become more specialised and graduate to Olympic lifting, you are trying to improve mainly on two lifts and you can concentrate on these. You must use other exercises to assist you in this aim, but your repertoire is considerably reduced so you must phase your work to do the correct thing at the right time. More will be said about this later.

Theoretically it may be better that the schedule be changed gradually and become progressively harder week by week and change to a new schedule, in stages, rather than have a completely new workout all at one time. This would prevent quite a lot of aches and pains on changing to a new routine and would be more scientific, but in practice, an enthusiast gets a great fillip from a new schedule and the very aches and pains mentioned are proof to him that he is working out in a different way which should improve him still further. There will undoubtedly be numerous questions on compiling schedules running through your mind after this brief introduction to the subject, and I hope that the answers to many of these will be covered in the rest of this section.

Keeping records

It is absolutely essential that training be properly recorded if it is to be successful. Notes on all workouts should be kept in training diaries, log books, etc. These show which methods produce the best results and allow future programmes to be made up accordingly. Involvement in serious competitive lifting means that you must not only keep notes of all workouts, but you should record every workout lift by lift. All the great champions do this, and it is amazing how useful these notes can be. I have frequently referred back to previous competitions to see how lifters tapered off, how their weight reduced etc.; all these little notes help you with preparation.

The best clubs have a card system filed in proper drawers; members get their card on entry to the gym and it is filed as they leave after the workout. Others have a rack on to which the lifters pin their workouts. A properly controlled system is to be highly recommended and I suggest having a training record book some sample pages of which are shown on page 54.

Split workouts

Split routines are for the truly dedicated enthusiast whether he is a weightlifter, power lifter or bodybuilder, and I will go as far as to say that few men will reach the top of their sphere nowadays unless they use split workouts of one kind or another. The reason for this is not hard to find. To become a champion in these days of extremely high standards means working-out many days a week. The conventional three days a week with a rest day in between is fine for most folks, but to get right to the top, five or even six times weekly training is very necessary. Success is built on the 'overload' principle, that training must always get progressively harder, but the muscle must have a certain amount of rest in between and to work the same muscle groups each day and on consecutive days is just asking for staleness and with it a termination of progress. To get over this, **split routines** are introduced so that very hard work is done on one part of the body in one workout and the next one a completely different area is attacked. So although there is no conventional 'rest period', individual body parts **are** being rested. This is an oversimplification of the theory, but it certainly points to the principle.

It is a suitable system for the man who can only spare three nights a week to train in club but wishes to do some extra work at home. In this case he should do most of the heavy work in the gym and on the other days work out on lighter exercises. A weekly programme could be as follows:

**Schedule 1   Monday,
              Wednesday and**

	Friday (this is the main workout)
Schedule 2	Tuesday and Saturday
Rest	Thursday and Sunday

Very often lifters are afraid to decrease the volume of training during the month of the competition, thinking they will not be in good form. This is wrong; work must be tapered off in volume before major competitions, but it is equally wrong to taper off for minor competitions.

Staleness

I am often asked about staleness, its effects, and the remedy for it. This is not an easy subject; many coaches feel it is a psychological as much as a physiological matter, but I will give my personal views, based on experience and study over the years.

Staleness is usually thought of as the phenomenon evident when progress slows down and halts and performance sometimes even worsens. The lifter invariably demonstrates lethargy and a lack of enthusiasm.

There are several reasons for staleness but it is most common when the lifter tries to gain too quickly, work too hard and maintain a peak for too long a period. This does not mean the solution is to take it easy. On the contrary, the lifter must work very hard, but it must be the **right kind of work at the right time.** He must resist the natural tendency to continually try to surpass his previous best; staleness results when mental demands exceed physical capabilities.

Excess efforts lead to aimless, or non-productive muscular contractions which override the coordination and reflex actions necessary for smooth performances.

There is also a danger of staleness when skill training is continued for too long. Acquisition of skill allows work to be performed with less effort, so a gain in skill without a corresponding increase in intensity or volume of work results eventually in poorer physical condition.

The symptoms

Apart from a loss of form, there may also be a disinclination to train, diminished appetite and insomnia. Weight tends to fluctuate. Usually, there are only one or two of these symptoms, depending on the degree of staleness.

The remedy

A change of work is the best remedy but the 'butterfly' complex, with constant changes of schedules, should be avoided. I firmly believe that the best way to avoid staleness is **long-term planning** with phased training covering fitness, strength and technique on the lines advocated in this book. This gives controlled and calculated variety. It allows for a seasonal dropping off from peak form, well away from the major competitions.

By varying the nature of your work in this way, by varying poundages in terms of intensity and volume in accordance with a long-term plan, staleness should become a rarity.

A Soviet viewpoint

The Russians maintain, and I agree with them, that you will not achieve maximum results unless there is a good decrease of volume as the major contest approaches. Likewise, frequent tapering off will lead to a repeating of the same results in each contest instead of a big total at the major one. The Soviet coaches believe that essentials for good planning of volumes and intensity are systematic medical super-

Sultan Rakhmanov, super- heavyweight Olympic champion. A typical product of the Soviet system

vision and the good health of the weightlifter.

In annual training, physical preparation other than weightlifting is necessary. This means morning exercises must be done for approximately 20 minutes each day or 120 hours annually. There must also be swimming, skipping, light athletics, etc. (depending on the seasons), 1 hour, three times weekly (12 hours monthly) in the second period. This is approximately 125 hours in the year. If we add to these a common physical preparation, then 350 hours must be done annually. (We take this to mean weightlifting exercises.) For special physical preparation, 520 hours must be done annually which is about 40 per cent of training.

Long-term planning

If lifters are to reach their full potential, long-term planning is absolutely essential. Many coaches and performers never look beyond their current schedule. In the very highest circles of the sport, at top international level, some coaches claim they have four-year plans, but a great many have two-year schemes of work and nearly all good coaches suggest that at least one-year plans are followed. This means that the schedules for a whole year should be considered right from the beginning of the year and the major competition should be the end product of the twelve month period of training. For some lifters, this will only be an area championship, but for great competitors, it will be the world championships, and with these top men, their own national championships, international matches, etc. must take second place. In Olympic years, even a Continental championship — such as the European championships — must take second place because in these circumstances it is not the highest 'peak' of the year. It can readily be understood that it is virtually impossible for someone of world class to do top totals several times a year and still continue to progress each time.

Every four years lifters in Britain find themselves having to compete in area championships to qualify for the British championships; they then have the national competitions to qualify for the Commonwealth Games; a few months later the World championships come along. Something has to suffer; several lifters show varying results and take it rather easy in the less important events. If maximum results are attempted too often and training tapered off and broken for each competition, it is inevitable that progress will suffer — there may even be retrogression in the long run.

While it is permissible to compete in various events, there should not be any undue tapering off or break in training. For top men, major contests should be limited to three or four per year but competitors at area and national levels can participate in around six each year.

This type of training builds a plateau of physical fitness on to which an experienced coach can put a psychological peak and also a physical peak by the tapering-off process.

How to make up and record an annual plan

First of all, you must decide if two peaks or one peak is to be the aim. Personally, I consider the ideal to be one principal peak and one subsidiary peak, thus the annual plan consists of **two** cycles of training. These are similar in character but

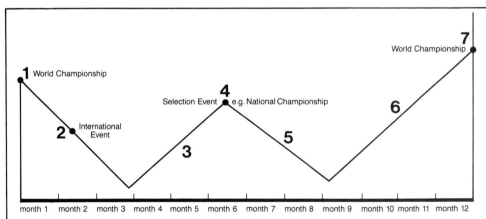

A one-year competition preparation schedule.
Although the example shows a world championship target the formula can be adapted for national, regional or other competitions.
1. The cycle starts after a world championship.
2. The descending line indicates the tapering off, active rest and fitness work period, possibly taking in an international team event or a match of lesser importance.
3. This is the build up towards a selection event for the next major championship, so leads to a subsidiary, rather than the main, peak.
4. An event at which the selection is made for the premier event of the year.
5. Tapering off, active rest, fitness work, etc., after selection.
6. The major build up of the year.
7. The highest point in the year's training programme. Obviously, you are aiming for continual improvement, so the build up ends at a higher point than the previous year.

with the second (and main cycle) being more intensive.

The first stage of planning is a systematic review of the situation. How much can be attained in view of the person's age, amount and nature of previous training, amount of time at present available, other commitments such as business and family, how much motivation there is, level of opposition, etc., etc. All these must influence decisions. You must then look at past and current results. Are there any particular weaknesses? Can a record be set in any lift? Even an area or national record would help provide motivation and assist training for top performers. Schedules will be composed with these special weaknesses and/or strengths in mind. Many sportsmen I meet in clubs just use standard schedules without any adaptations for these factors. The schedules which will be outlined, are for average, fairly well balanced enthusiasts, but schedules should be adjusted as outlined above.

While competition results provide the ultimate test of training methods, it is necessary to look wider than this to see if overall progress is being made.

The strength lifts, the fundamental exercises and athletic training will give a first class indication of results **providing good records are kept.** If training shows little or no progress, then there is

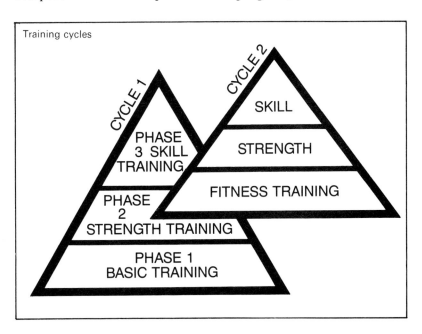

Training cycles

CYCLE 1

CYCLE 2

SKILL

PHASE 3 SKILL TRAINING

STRENGTH

PHASE 2

FITNESS TRAINING

STRENGTH TRAINING

PHASE 1 BASIC TRAINING

something lacking in the training plan or its application in the gym. In the training log book, there should be a note of the results on the lines illustrated. Keep an eye on these records over a long period and you will be surprised at how revealing they can be.

A comparison of strength type lifts with the best snatch and jerk is also well worth while. Philip Guenov, the Bulgarian coach, told me of some very systematic research done to discover the inter-dependence between assistance exercises and the three Olympic lifts. The results of this experiment and research enable us to estimate whether more pure strength work should be done or whether speed and technique exercises would be more beneficial. A good balance is essential and the reasons for this will be obvious to any clear-thinking coach. The figures suggested in the following guide are based on the lengthy and methodical research mentioned earlier.

A simplified form of record keeping

	Cycle 1	Cycle 2	Cycle 1	Cycle 2
Snatch				
Clean and jerk				
Front squat				
High pull with grip				
to standing belt height				
100 metres time				
Vertical jump				

Date	Time from: until:	Body weight	Remarks					
Exercise	Weight/reps			Total sets	Total reps	Intensity	Average intensity	Total tonnage
front squat	$\frac{90}{5}$ $\frac{105}{4}$ $\frac{115}{3}$ $\frac{120}{3}$			*4*	*15*	*120*	*105*	*1575*

It is a good idea to keep your own log book. 'Average intensity' is calculated by dividing the weight by the number of repetitions

54

They will show where assistance is not required.

Back squat — good balance = 35kg more than clean. If only 27·5kg more than clean then strength rather than technique training is needed.

Front squat — good balance = 15kg more than clean. If only 10kg more, then work on strength. If 20kg more, then technique work on clean required.

Obviously with training you can squat with fantastic poundages compared with what you can pull in for the clean, but providing you can do a squat (with feet in the same position as you would rise from in a clean) with 42.5kg (say 95lb) more than you can pull in, then you have an adequate reserve of leg strength. Where the squat is much more, you could profitably spend time on other types of work. The reverse also holds true.

A systematic review of plans and weaknesses is just the starting point. The next step is to make out a systematic phased programme. This is what I would consider a first-class phased programme. I call this **pyramid training** because it first builds for the lifter a broad base of fitness and then leads him upwards to the peak of physical perfection and top totals. Obviously **mental** conditioning is also necessary but this will be discussed separately.

Pyramid training

Fitness is, of course, very specific.

Many champion lifters are not 'fit' in the widely accepted athletic meaning. Certainly they are fit for weightlifting and they are very strong, but in many cases there is room for considerable improvement in efficiency of heart, lungs, co-ordination, etc. They may be well above average compared with most men, but if maximum potential is desired, something more is called for and a lifter should have a phase of training where real fitness is built. Not only does this give a welcome change of routine, which does physical good, it is also psychologically sound and alleviates staleness. It gives a real solid base for continued progress and helps the body recover faster from effort.

Your training year may be divided into one or two pyramids, depending on your competitive programme and how far apart you intend to make your 'peaks'.

Many sports have two major competitions annually so two peaks are desirable, but if you have a preliminary selection followed by just one major competition one pyramid would be more suitable. The length of each phase will be determined by whether there

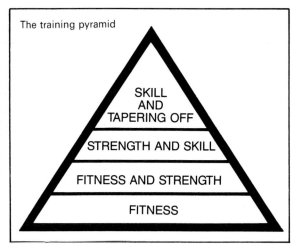

The training pyramid

SKILL
AND
TAPERING OFF

STRENGTH AND SKILL

FITNESS AND STRENGTH

FITNESS

are one or two pyramids. If there is one pyramid the phasing will be roughly as follows:

Phase 1 (fitness) — 3 months
Phase 2 (fitness and strength) — 3 months
Phase 3 (strength and skill) — 3 months
Phase 4 (skill, tapering off, competitions and short rest) — 3 months

If it is a **double pyramid** then this is the build-up:

Phase 1   6 weeks
Phase 2   6 weeks
Phase 3   8 weeks
Phase 4   6 weeks (three weeks mainly skill, two weeks tapering off and contest, one week rest)

Bulgarian research indicates that **intensity** of training is more important than simply **tonnage** (volume). In the long term, better results will be obtained by increasing tonnage via increased intensity. In fact, Abadejev increased his team's tonnage by 50 per cent in six years. General tonnage is easily improved by spending more time lifting and the Bulgarians often lift twice daily, three times weekly, and once only on the other two days. The Bulgarian lifters work much harder than those in other countries. They often train with weights five to six times a week and more. They use a greater volume and intensity than is the case in other countries; perhaps because they have better conditions and less problems in earning a living. They use about 10 per cent higher intensity in pulls and squats than the Soviet lifters and at an International Training Conference in Sofia it was revealed that Bulgarian lifters trained as much as 25 hours a week, with a weekly volume of up to 96 tonnes and a monthly volume of 360-370 tonnes, e.g.

Monday	**25 tonnes**
Tuesday	**12 tonnes**
Wednesday	**22 tonnes**
Friday	**27 tonnes**
Saturday	**10 tonnes**

This regime lasts for three weeks and a lighter fourth week has the following tonnage:

Monday	**15 tonnes**
Tuesday	**7 tonnes**
Wednesday	**15 tonnes**
Thursday	**active rest**
Friday	**19 tonnes**
Saturday	**6 tonnes**
Sunday	**active rest**

How much training?

Good lifting technique is extremely important but the lifter's physical fitness and training background play an equally important role. We are fortunate in our sport that we can keep very precise records and adopt a very methodical approach where progression is measurable and apparent. Unfortunately not enough attention is given to an organised programme or sound planning.

In lifting we can measure the weight lifted in a single lift, in a competition total, calculate numbers of lifts and training loads which can be indicated in pounds, foot-pounds or tons. Clearly, the effect of lifting 250kg once is very different from that of lifting 50kg five times: the first has a much higher **intensity.** Among knowledgeable lifters and coaches, there is now a fairly widely accepted approach and terminology and this can be explained as follows:

Volume (sometimes called total training load or tonnage)

We usually specify training loads in kilograms or tonnes and this shows how much the lifter totals in a training session, week, month or year. You simply sum (add together) every lift regardless

Dragnev of Bulgaria, 1985 junior World champion. An example of the Bulgarian training system

of which kind of movement it represents. Obviously there is a difference between a 'short' movement (heel raise or shoulder shrug) and a 'large' movement such as a snatch, so if you want to be really precise you can measure foot pounds, i.e. you can multiply the weight in each lift by the height lifted. However, in practice most coaches are agreed that it is sufficient simply to work in total **tonnage** by obtaining the sum total of all weights in all repetitions.

Intensity

This is calculated by taking the total training load in a workout, week, month etc. and dividing it by the total number of repetitions during the same period. You can also use this to calculate the intensity of a single exercise e.g. if in snatching workout you do 140 × 3, 150 × 3, 160 × 3, 170 × 2, 180 × 2, 190 × 1, 200 × 1, the calculations are as follows:

Total repetitions 15.

$$140 × 3 = 420$$
$$150 × 3 = 450$$
$$160 × 3 = 480$$
$$170 × 2 = 340$$
$$180 × 2 = 360$$
$$190 × 1 = 190$$
$$200 × 1 = 200$$

$$2,440$$

2,440 divided by 15 = 163 approx.

This is the average intensity. You should also take note of the number of lifts done in the snatch or clean and jerk with over 90 per cent of the present best competitive lifts as this will help prepare workouts and competition attempts. All this, even the failures (with a stroke through the weight) should be recorded in your training diary.

Light, medium and heavy training

Training is classed as **heavy** if 9 or more tonnes are lifted in a session (although obviously the lifter's bodyweight has a bearing on the subject). With this range, the higher the intensity the heavier the workout. Training is also heavy if there is a large number of lifts with 90 per cent or over in the workout.

A **medium** workout would be 6 to 9 tonnes and a **light** workout would be 4.5 to 6 tonnes.

Heavy training gets the best results but it takes the body a week or 10 days to fully recover from a heavy workout and to gain the quickest results, one must train with medium and light loads during the recovery period.

Soviet champions, with their fantastic medical back-up to properly monitor recuperation and guard against over-training, sometimes do two or even three heavy workouts in a row to get maximum effect and then taper off with three or four lighter workouts.

Novices and lighter weights train alternately on snatch and clean doing only one of these in each workout. In the heavier classes they often do these lifts only once a week and then not in the same workout. An interesting point, demon-strating the importance of keeping a balanced view of the subject, is put forward by Dr Mikhailov, USSR weightlifting physiologist: 'To improve results in the snatch you must reduce intensities in all movements, even in assistance work; but improvement of clean and jerk results requires heavy training weights.'

Length of workout

The more experienced the lifter the longer the workout may be. An hour is too much for the complete novice but after a very short time one to one-and-a-half hours is correct. The heaviest, most experienced men may go to three hours on occasion but that depends on whether or not they do physical work to earn a living.

Systematic improvement

Everybody knows that weightlifting is the most progressive form of training, for in nearly every workout the trainee tries to increase either the poundage handled or the number of repetitions or sets. We are great advocates of such progression. The Soviet coaches have shown us another way to estimate the amount of work. Never let it be said that we have a system which is all our own work — certainly we may have a unique system, but it is unique only insofar as we have tried to take the most successful factors from other training schemes and adapt them to our own.

The concept I present now is the theory of **total work output**. The further you progress up the ladder towards world-class performance the more useful the theory becomes but even the least experienced will find it useful to see how much work they are doing compared with others. It is not always the man who lifts the heaviest weights who does the most work!

The Russians call it the **load volume,** although sometimes they speak of the **load** or the **volume**. We talk about the **tonnage** and mean the same thing as load volume. The load volume, however, is not the only thing which must be considered or else the man in our sample schedule could do numerous repetitions with light weights and get the same end tonnage. The intensity must be carefully graded. Most novices want to keep increasing the poundage of their maximum training lifts and this will often ruin technique, hinder progress, cause staleness and even result in injury. The wise coach will **gradually** increase the volume by adding a repetition here and sticking on weight there — thus the tyro is still progressing yet hardly notices the extra work. In your training book you should always keep an eye on the tonnage and intensity. Keep in mind that the 'light' squat or dead lifts can add to tonnage without being intensive so you must not fool yourself with such poundages. Label your exercises 'light', 'medium' or 'heavy'. 80 per cent or more of your maximum can be classed as heavy. Around 75 per cent is medium. I would class light weights as about 50 per cent of maximum. The next question likely to be asked is; 'What total tonnage should be used?' The answer is not easy but briefly it depends first on the length of time you have been training and, secondly, on which stage of training you are at — how near you are to a contest. The tonnage will be greatest in the strength and power training period of a phased programme. It will also be high in the middle of the phase where you are concentrating on the Olympic lifts themselves, but then, as you increase intensity (by virtue of higher poundages in single or low repetitions) the tonnage will begin to decrease. When you are tapering off, your tonnage is lower still.

This should provide a good general guide; more specifically, here are some figures on **tonnage** or **total work output.**

Vorobiev, the Soviets' chief National Coach, says that their top lifters rarely handle more than 115 tonnes in a month. Knowing the Russian system very well and knowing how and when they train, we can say this would include about 27 sessions of which 5 would be very heavy.

Going from the sublime to the ridiculous I can see now that although I was considered to be a hard worker in my own competitive days, I actually did not train hard enough. I did not lift enough tonnes in a workout to reach my true potential. My heaviest Olympic workouts were around 3.6 tonnes and this included a tonne of squats. I probably used heavier workouts in power lifting competitions! Of course it is quite in order for your tonnage to drop as a contest approaches owing to the change of workouts. Your tonnage will drop by around 25-35 per cent. This is because you are dropping many of the heavy assistance exercises and increasing the intensity of the snatch and jerk. In the tapering off phase it will drop even more. You will reach your heaviest workout about two weeks before the event, then your tonnage takes about a 25 per cent drop with the taper-off so it will seem very low in comparison with your top tonnages in the strengthening phase. This is in order because intensity is high but you must also now start to build up a reserve of energy even with these high intensity workouts. Be sure that at the end of every session you enter in your training book the tonnage you use. It will take only a few minutes to calculate it and then you will see immediately if you are improving and if and when you change your routines you will not be so likely to make mistakes.

Vorobyev: a former champion, now a successful coach

In the **tonnage progression programme** (page 62) you will see that the lifter is working to approximately 90 per cent of maximum. This has little increase in intensity but the tonnage has increased from 775kg to 1222·5kg.

From this stage you may wish to continue adding tonnage but also increase intensity. For this purpose, I have devised another special schedule — a **dual tonnage and intensity progress schedule.** There is a danger of changing the nature of the schedule if numerous sets of four repetitions are introduced; adjustments have to be made to retain the main characteristics.

This programme must not be in any way rushed. The very subtle increase of work is hardly noticeable, but you will see by the tonnage that there has been a considerable increase during the period. This is not by any means over-ambitious, for although there are about 18 increases detailed over the 2 previous schedules you are not once asked to lift more than your initial maximum, i.e. 110kg. Of course 110kg will no longer be your maximum. These schedules will have increased it and you still have not been working at maximum intensity. As the season progresses and the major competitions approach, you will wish to increase the intensity of your workouts by adding more weight and using heavier poundages, even if it means cutting down on tonnage. The **intensity progression programme** (page 63) is slanted towards this aim, and yet maintaining a balance of work to hold the gains you have already made.

It is interesting to note that there have been intensity and volume increases in all sets except the first and the drop of 25kg in total tonnage, compared with the target of the last schedule, is due simply to the fact that a single repetition has been dropped from the first set. If this had been left at 4 repetitions there would be a tonnage increase rather than a decrease.

These three programmes spread over a considerable period should add many pounds to your best lift. You may wish to set them out in your training book something like this, but with your personal poundages and targets, and tick them off as you attain your aims.

Tonnage progression programme (in kg)

Starting point	70 × 2	80 × 2	90 × 2	95 × 1	100 × 1 + 1	
Progression 1	70 × 3	80 × 2	90 × 2	95 × 1	100 × 1 + 1	
Progression 2	70 × 3	80 × 3	90 × 2	95 × 1	100 × 1 + 1	
Progression 3	70 × 3	80 × 3	90 × 3	95 × 1	100 × 1 + 1	
Progression 4	70 × 3	80 × 3	90 × 3	95 × 2	100 × 1 + 1	
Progression 5	70 × 3	80 × 3	90 × 3	95 × 2	100 × 2 + 1	
Target	70 × 3	80 × 3	90 × 3	95 × 2	100 × 2 + 2	102·5 × 1

Dual tonnage and intensity progress schedule (in kg)

Starting point	70 × 3	80 × 3	90 × 3	95 × 2	100 × 2	102 × 1 + 1 = 1314kg	
Progression 1	70 × 4	80 × 3	90 × 3	95 × 2	100 × 2	102 × 1 + 1	
Progression 2	72 × 4	80 × 3	90 × 3	95 × 2	100 × 2	102 × 1 + 1	
Progression 3	72 × 4	80 × 4	90 × 3	95 × 2	100 × 2	102 × 1 + 1	
Progression 4	72 × 4	82 × 3	90 × 3	95 × 2	100 × 2	102 × 1 + 1	
Progression 5	72 × 4	82 × 3	90 × 4	95 × 2	100 × 2	102 × 1 + 1	
Progression 6	72 × 4	82 × 3	92 × 3	95 × 2	100 × 2	102 × 1 + 1	
Progression 7	72 × 4	82 × 3	92 × 3	95 × 3	100 × 2	102 × 1 + 1	
Progression 8	72 × 4	82 × 3	92 × 3	97 × 2	100 × 2	102 × 1 + 1	
Progression 9	72 × 4	82 × 3	92 × 3	97 × 2	102 × 2	102 × 1 + 1 + 1	
Progression 10	72 × 4	82 × 3	92 × 3	97 × 2	102 × 2	105 × 1	
Progression 11	72 × 4	82 × 3	92 × 3	97 × 2	102 × 2	105 × 1	
Target	72 × 4	82 × 3	92 × 3	97 × 2	102 × 2	105 × 1	107 × 1 + 1 = 1527kg

Intensity progression programme (in kg)

Starting point	72 × 3	82 × 3	92 × 3	97 × 2	102 × 2	105 × 1	107 × 1 + 1
Progression 1	75 × 3	82 × 3	92 × 3	97 × 2	102 × 2	105 × 1	107 × 1 + 1
Progression 2	75 × 3	85 × 3	92 × 3	97 × 2	102 × 2	105 × 1	107 × 1 + 1
Progression 3	75 × 3	85 × 3	95 × 3	97 × 2	102 × 2	105 × 1	107 × 1 + 1
Progression 4	75 × 3	85 × 3	95 × 3	100 × 2	102 × 2	105 × 1	107 × 1 + 1
Progression 5	75 × 3	85 × 3	95 × 3	100 × 2	105 × 2	105 × 2	107 × 1 + 1
Progression 6	75 × 3	85 × 3	95 × 3	100 × 2	105 × 2 + 2	105 × 1	107 × 1 + 1
Progression 7	75 × 3	85 × 3	95 × 3	100 × 2	105 × 2	107 × 1	110 × 1
Target	75 × 3	85 × 3	95 × 3	100 × 2	105 × 2	107 × 1	110 × 1 + 1

Starting tonnage = 1455kg
Finishing tonnage = 1502kg
Main increase is in **intensity**.

Phased training

It can be seen that in this book the wide view, the overall approach, is used because I strongly believe the novice should be taught good technique from the start and that long-term planning is absolutely essential for all lifters. Most of the principles and methods outlined are as applicable to the weightlifting 'rabbit' as they are to the 'tigers' of the platform **but the degree of work varies considerably**. Weightlifters can expect a long competitive life, unlike the little swimming or gymnastic girls who are world champions while they are still at school and over the hill by the time they are old enough to vote! This long competitive life calls for a special approach: a competitor will normally only carry on whilst he is still making progress, and yet as a man reaches maturity many external factors tend to impede progress. This section aims at prolonging improvement in competition results. It is a fine sport that can boast of having world class competitors from the ages of 13 to 40+, with fathers and sons competing together.

The fact that in many cases progress slows or halts after 10 or 20 years' hard training is caused not so much by age as by the fact that the body has adjusted itself almost fully to the work placed before it. One of the basic requirements for mature lifters, therefore, is a change of routine in a shorter period than would normally be the case. Changes of intensity are advocated as well as changes of exercise and tempo. The advanced weightlifter should do a considerable number of sets using 5 to 6 repetitions, particularly if trying to gain muscle mass in the right places for weightlifting results. There is also a place in the routine for some isometric work. As lifters reach their thirties and even forties there should be a decreasing of work, but do not assume that 'older' necessarily means 'advanced'. Nowadays we get some very advanced young lifters.

67-77 per cent of maximum and weights of this calibre should be used in more than half of all lifts. This fine coach also recommended the following optimum training weights for assistance exercises (the percentage applying to the snatch or clean and jerk as appropriate):

Power snatch with dip (from hang, blocks or platform)	62-72% of snatch
Power snatch without dip	57-67% of snatch
Dead lift wide grip	85-167% of snatch
Power pull wide grip	80-95% of snatch
Stiff leg dead lift wide grip	85-100% of snatch
Power clean with dip	62-72% of clean
Power jerk	62-72% of jerk
Dead lift normal grip	80-92% of clean
Power pull (blocks) normal grip	85-100% of clean
Squats	75-110% of best clean and jerk weight

There should not be more than 7 different exercises in a routine and there may well be as little as 3 if these lifts are being done thoroughly. The total repetitions for a 7 exercise schedule should not exceed 100 and a full week's repetitions should not normally exceed 230.

In the snatch and the clean and jerk there will probably be 8 to 16 lifts in a workout with 5 to 6 additions of weights, but remember, variety in the volume of training is very important to advanced lifters. Falameev of the USSR recommends that the optimum training weight in the snatch and clean and jerk should be

It is very seldom that weights of over 100 per cent are used nowadays as it has been found that although there are gains of strength speed diminishes.

With the various guidelines given, it should now be a simple matter to compile result-producing schedules and the good thing about this approach is that there is great scope for personal choice. This inbuilt flexibility gives coaches and lifters lots of freedom for individual preferences, which I am sure will be welcomed by all advanced and experienced performers. One final word of warning; you will prefer the work which you do best, but if you want continued progress, concentrate on your weaknesses.

Phase 1 — Fitness

A whole thesis could be written on why fitness is necessary and in fact this very problem was tackled extremely systematically by my great friend, the late John P. Jesse of California who reviewed most of the good existing literature on the subject and proved conclusively that lifters can expect higher totals if they make fitness work an integral part of their scheme. John P. Jesse showed that heart and lung efficiency will allow the performer to train harder, recover quicker and perform better under competition conditions — whether it is a short competition with only a single warm-up or a lengthy contest, like major championships with large entries, requiring the contestants to warm up for individual lifts.

The physiological side of this type of work is beyond our scope here, so I will confine myself to recommending workouts and basic principles to produce maximum fitness. **Fartlek training** and **interval running** are among the most popular means of producing cardio-vascular fitness, but I believe that this should be

approached slowly by those without at least some athletic background. Building to a peak must be a gradual process; build up progressively so that discomfort is kept to a minimum and, where possible, enjoyment is maximal. The best way to start then is with a routine something like this:

Early fitness work

Heart and lung work
1 **Walk 50 yards, run 100 yards**
2 **Walk 50 yards, run 150 yards**
3 **Walk 50 yards, run 200 yards**
4 **Walk 100 yards, run 250 yards**
5 **Walk 100 yards, run 300 yards**
6 **Walk 100 yards, run 350 yards**
7 **Walk 100 yards, run 400 yards**

You will see that if you are doing this on a quarter-mile track you have not at any time run even one full lap. Surely nobody can object to a programme like this! The total work, however, has built up well, and this is only a start. You must gradually increase the runs without increasing the walks and the runs must get faster too. If you are doing it in the gym, you may prefer to calculate in paces instead of

WARMING UP EXERCISES FREE STANDING

Wheel labels: TRUNK TWISTS, SIDE BENDS, ASTRIDE JUMPS, JUMP SQUATS, (1), (2), (3), (4)

	INTERVAL RUNNING	STANDING LONG JUMPS	INTERVAL RUNNING	WALKING
	① FAST & SLOW RUNS 50 YDS EACH ALTERNATELY TOTAL TIME 3 MINS	**②** 3 @ 50% EFFORT 3 @ 75% 3 @ 100%	**③** AS 1 TOTAL TIME 2 MINS	**④** RECOVERY PERIOD

Heart and lung fitness.
In the recovery period the lifter walks as a depletive to get his breathing back to normal before continuing with the schedule

Exercise	Day												
	1	2	3	4	5	6	7	8	9	10	11	12	13
Press & squat	12	13	14	15	15	16	17	17	18	18	19	20	20
Incline press	12	13	14	15	15	16	17	17	18	19	20	20	20
Clean high pulls	12	13	14	15	15	15	16	17	17	18	19	20	20
Hang snatch	10	11	12	12	13	14	15	16	17	18	19	20	20
Cleans	10	11	11	12	13	14	15	16	17	18	19	20	20
Jerks	12	13	14	14	15	15	16	16	17	18	19	20	20
Squats	15	15	15	15	16	16	17	18	18	19	19	20	20
Heel raise	15	16	16	17	18	18	19	19	19	20	20	20	20

Muscular endurance.
This schedule is based on the work of John P Jesse. On the first day 12 reps are done on the first three exercises, 10 on the next two, and so on. Over thirteen workouts you gradually increase to 20 reps on each exercise

yards, e.g. you walk 50 paces and then run 100, and so on.

This should be done three times weekly and should be followed by a free exercise flexibility routine designed to work all the muscles and joints through their full range. Arm, shoulder and chest exercises for four minutes, e.g. backward arm circles, alternate arm swings as far forward and far back as possible, forward circles and press-ups.

67

Waist and hip work
Sit-ups in sets of 20
Trunk circling, 12 repetitions
each way for 2 minutes
Jack-knife, 2 sets, 12 repetitions
Leg raises, 20 repetitions
Back, hip raises 15 repetitions
Leg work
Ankle-stretching, ankle-
circling
Standing long jumps, 4
maximum efforts
Consecutive long jumps, 3
close-footed long jumps, repeat
3 times
Vertical jump, 3 maximum
efforts in test style
Fast squats, 25 repetitions,
increase eventually to around
70 repetitions
Finish off with
supplementary recreational
work, e.g. if at home you should
do some simple forward rolls
or hand and head balancing; in
the gym or outdoors, partner
hand-balancing, agilities such
as hand springs, etc. and
whenever possible a proper
game. In order of priority, I
would recommend volleyball,
basketball, baseball, minor
team games and football.
Avoid contact sports and
anything with high injury
potential. You can also play
around with light weights but
play and **light** are the operative
words.

On other days more work
must be done. One should be
reserved for a fairly long walk,
cycling or swimming. The
advantage of these activities is
that you can make them social
occasions with family or
friends and at the same time
get the active yet relaxing type
of activity we are after.

The other day should be
reserved for a weight workout
using fairly light weights, e.g.
1 Skipping, 3 minutes
2 Snatch, 10 repetitions, 2 sets
3 Seated press, 10 repetitions, 3
   sets
4 Snatch without split or
   squat, 15 repetitions × 2 sets
5 Split jumps, 25 repetitions
6 Jerks. Use barbell equal to
   bodyweight, 2 sets with 6
   repetitions less than
   maximum weight for a single
   group plus one or two
   'tinkering' exercises of your
   choice.

Intermediate fitness work

Having followed this routine
for some four weeks (in a single
pyramid scheme) you are now
ready for some tougher
training on the fartlek system.
For this it is better to get out
into the country, in amongst
the woods and the fields, but if
you are in the centre of a city do
not let this stop you: there will
always be a football field, track
or even some waste ground
where you can run. I advocate
rough country so that you have
to vary your stride and
occasionally dodge and jump
obstacles, which avoids a

John McNiven, who has won more Scottish and British awards than any
other lifter

boring, mechanical rhythm. One of the most enjoyable periods of my own training days was when I trained on Sunday mornings with Highland Games athletes at the Bay of Nigg. We would go running along the cliffs, descend over rough boulders, run in the shingle; sand is also great to run in, it is tough and builds up stamina. We would climb and clamber, walk and run, swing over obstacles and finally swim in the sea. The sessions would finish off with about 10-15 sprints, ranging from 30-70 metres each.

These sprints were done like proper races. Someone would give the starts and we would really try to win over the distance, then have a slow walk back to the start and begin all over again.

This is the sort of programme I would recommend but I suggest you try to adjust this according to your circumstances and if you can do something like our Sunday sessions, you are on a real winner because it's great fun. We did this in summer and most of the winter. I have even been training on 1 January after a really hectic Scottish New Year. Do not let the weather put you off. Get wrapped up in a tracksuit and sweater and you'll be all right.

The following are guides to the sort of thing you should aim at:

10 minutes slow jogging, break for free exercises covering all parts of the body (say 7-8 minutes), 10 minutes medium jogging, slow down to a walk then gradually build up to a really tough pace for five minutes and slow down for a five-minute walk. Total time around 45 minutes at the most.

This should be followed by two all-out sprints at 50 metres and two very fast 100-metre sprints.

Throwing practice. Get a medicine ball or a small boulder. Practice double handed under-arm swing throws (4 half efforts then 3 all-out), then three all-out back over the head throws, also with two hands. If you have a special interest in any proper throwing events, this is the time to practise these.

Finally, some jumping should be done. If a pit is available do three long jumps and three hop, step and jumps with maximum speed run-ups. If there is no pit available try three maximum hops on each leg plus three maximum hop, step and jumps from the standing position. Watch that the heels do not become bruised. Well-padded insoles are advisable here.

This sort of routine should be done at least twice a week during this phase and I would suggest two outdoor workouts and two indoor workouts.

Circuit training

Circuit training may be included in the indoor sessions; here is a circuit suitable for our purposes. We should make full use of weightlifting apparatus as this will be readily available.

1 **Power clean**
2 **Heave jerks (no split)**
3 **Hyperextensions**
4 **Burpee jumps**
5 **Sit ups, to touch knees only**
6 **Squats**

Exercises 3, 4, and 5 are done without weights. The lifting exercises should be done with weights half your maximum single for the same movement. The exercises should be done ten times in each set. You work from exercise 1 to 6 then back to 1 again and repeat the whole sequence. It is then done a third time so that the total is three complete circuits. The whole routine is timed and you progress **not** by adding weight or increasing the repetitions, but by **reducing the time taken to perform the routine.**

Circuit training like this can be done three times weekly on alternate days. This is only part of your training — a component if you wish. Weight training now begins to play a more important part but it is still with very light weights. The idea of the next routine is to build endurance, so that the working muscles recover quickly from their tasks and the work capacity is increased. This will stand the trainee in good stead when he comes on to the strength, power and finally the competitive period.

The exercises should all be done for 2 sets of 25 repetitions and gradually increased to 30 repetitions. When 2 sets of 30 repetitions can be done with the poundage initially used, change to 3 sets of 25

1 **Dumb-bell press**
2 **Hang cleans**
3 **Dead lift**   **Alternate sets dead lifts done bending knees, not stiff leg style**

4 **Bench press**
5 **Leg press**   **Alternate sets**
6 **Pullovers at arms length**
7 **Lateral raise**   **Sequence training**
8 **Leg raise**   **Do one set of each exercise**
9 **Heel raise**   **non-stop if possible (if not**
10 **Abdominal raise**   **possible with minimum of delay) then repeat sequence again, i.e. Ex. 7, 8, 9, 10, 7, 8, 9, 10**

repetitions and gradually work to 3 sets of 30 repetitions. Keep the rest pause between groups as short as possible. The state of your breathing provides a good guide. Although you will be breathless immediately after each set this will not last and your breathing should return to normal after two minutes. If still very short of breath, delay the start of the set. It should never be more than three minutes between sets; one and a half or two minutes is much better. The sequence of 4 exercises should be done with little or no pause between sets. If you are using a 3-month fitness phase you will now be ready for a real hard final 'bash'.

You will be working 5 days each week and attending the gym at least 3 times each week.

Your running and jumping workouts will be more intensive and weights will be getting a bit heavier and circuits more severe. Here are your final schedules for the fitness phase.

Advanced fitness work

A more intensive system is now introduced. This is known as **interval running** and the use of a stopwatch is to be highly recommended if you are to do this systematically. If you cannot lay your hands on one I suggest that you run the various distances at nearly top speed. Human nature being what it is you are unlikely to work so hard if you are not being timed.

1 **50 metres (approx. 8 sec) plus one minute walk back to the start and ready to repeat. Repeat 6 times.**
2 **100 metres (approx. 15 sec) plus one minute walk back to the start and ready to repeat. Repeat 6 times.**
3 **100 metres medium effort plus one minute walk back to the start and ready to repeat. Repeat 5 times.**
4 **100 metres slow pace, plus one minute walk back to the start and ready to repeat. Repeat 4 times.**
5 **100 metres fast pace, 1½ minutes recovery. Repeat 4 times.**
6 **220 metres fast, 2 min to recover. Repeat 3 times.**
7 **One slow 440 metre jogtrot.**

I know lifters will find this a rather hard schedule but it is easy compared with those of track and field athletes and very much easier than those advised by weightlifting coaches in Eastern bloc countries!

This workout should be done twice each week for the last month of the fitness phase.

Jumping movements will now be included in circuit and weight workouts but once weekly, maximum standing long and vertical jumps should be done and records kept of results.

Here is another circuit for twice-weekly practice at this phase of training.

Cheating curl
Seated press
Harvard steps
Jack knife
Squat jumps
Downward pulls with expander (or pull ups or pulley pull downs) 10-12 repetitions each. Really go for time improvement over the three times through the circuit. Finally, your weightlifting workout.

Knowing lifters as I do I am sure they will want to try some heavy lifting even during the fitness phase. I think these wishes must be accommodated; even in Russia it has been known for lifters to break into the gym in order to try heavy weights when advised against it! We must be systematic about heavy work and I suggest that during the fitness phase you limit heavy attempts to four evenly spaced heavy workouts. In these workouts you can go high on three or four movements, e.g. the two Olympics and a high pull or perhaps the main lifts plus a squat and a pull. All other work should be along the lines given below. Here is your final fitness routine with weights still working on the principles outlined before. Research shows that 'fitness' is specific; you may be very 'fit' in some ways but not for other things. We are wanting **lifting** fitness and this schedule will give this quality.

Press and squat
High pulls
Snatch from hang
Snatch without splitting or squatting
Cleans
Jerks
Squats
Fast heel raises (donkey style)
Slow, round back, dead lifts

Do twenty repetitions of each exercise. Whilst they must be done continuously there is no need for excessive speed, although only the dead lift should be done slowly. You will, perhaps, be surprised to find that fairly respectable weights can be handled for twenty repetitions in some of the exercises. Some of them, however, will have you gasping for breath even with light weights so just take it easy and work for the full twenty repetitions. Although we are still after efficiency of the heart and lungs, **muscular** endurance is the main object here and by the end of the fitness phase we should have a lifter who is super fit specifically for weightlifting and ready to build real strength and power on to his improved fitness level. Light weights and high repetitions like these are necessary from a physiological point of view to produce a chemical reaction in the muscles which makes the fast twitch muscles fibres take over from the slow twitch ones and this is vital for Olympic lifters. Assistance work can produce these beneficial physiological characteristics. This should not be applied to the two Olympic lifts themselves as light weights produce different movement patterns; in any case, skill lessens with the onset of fatigue so you would **not** be improving technique. On the contrary, you could be damaging it.

In the final fitness phase, group balancing and elementary tumbling is still advocated; games playing is also highly desirable. The standard of skill in these activities is not important; it is the physical effect that interests us. Those walks and sport with the family are also useful so make a habit of them. You will be all the better physically, more relaxed mentally and more popular with friends and family too, for later when it comes to the heavier stuff you will have little time or energy for such activities.

The sort of sports you should consider for this dual purpose (physical and social) work include tennis, squash, cycling, swimming, badminton, walking, hill walking and horse riding. I am not in favour of skiing because of the risk of injury and also warn against contact sports for similar reasons. Wrestling, boxing, rugby, judo and American football are good examples of the sort of thing I think **competitive** lifters should avoid.

You will notice that I have given guidance not only on the type of work but also on the amount and how many times weekly it should be done, although, being quite specific, it will be easy for coaches and lifters to adapt if they feel necessary; notice also how you can choose the distribution of your workouts. For example, you may wish to do circuit training in conjunction with your gym nights, or you may wish to make this a short home training workout. All this is possible under the scheme and I can see no earthly reason why it should not be followed closely. Fitness is the most neglected phase of training in most countries, particularly Britain and America, and it is the aspect in which Poland, Russia, Bulgaria and other top weightlifting countries shine.

Take the hint and make this an integral part of your annual training plan.

Phase 2 — Fitness and strength

After the basic conditioning schedules have been done, the lifter should move on to the strength phase. Remember that in a single pyramid year this strengthening period will last for about three months and in a double pyramid programme the strength phases will last about six weeks, but be repeated twice annually. This is a very important part of the training. I have seen unfit men win weightlifting competitions, I have seen lifters win with very poor technique, but I have yet to see anyone win a weightlifting event without **great strength.** This is the one department where there is always room for improvement.

Probably the greatest strides in strength development in post-war years were made by the Hungarians. From being a nation of nonentities in the weightlifting world, they suddenly became prominent and in a couple of years produced greats like Toth, Veres, Foldi, Nemmisanyi, Ecser, Nagy, Huska — I could go on and on. These men had two things in common: they had tremendous strength, and they became champions in spite of their technique rather than because of it. I always found their style abominable yet I was forced to admit they got good totals — **all because of strength and power.** Just imagine how great they would have been had they had good technique too! Nemmisanyi made his jerks without even splitting; Huska made every mistake in the book yet gave the world champions great competition; so it goes on. Two men seem to have been the main masterminds behind the Hungarian system, Veres and Bakos. I do not mean to

Alan McMahon doing a front squat during the strength phase of a long-term programme

Foldi — a product of the Hungarian strength building system. He is being meticulous about the placing of his hands on the bar

indicate they worked together, indeed I think they were rivals in the field. Veres's schedule was well tried in other countries and produced excellent results. It did, however, tend to make several top lifters put on extra weight — a consideration which must be kept in mind. Veres himself went up from middleweight to mid-heavy, although he lifted mostly in the light-heavies. An adaptation of this schedule, used by Toth (who took over the mid-heavyweight world title in 1966) was made popular in Germany through the medium of Wolfgang Peter, the German coach. It is because of its success that strength recommendations based on Hungarian principles became popular.

The exercises and workouts can, of course, be varied, but the key factors should remain unaltered. In strength and power training really heavy weights are used in exercises such as squatting, high pulls with clean and also snatch grips, heave jerks, power cleans, etc. These are all movements where technique is not so important as sheer hard work and constant effort. The number of workouts during the week will be changed from time to time, but in the really

apart of course. I would have thought one could get very stale with the same or very similar workouts during the year, but I assure you this is what the information from Hungary shows. We advocate that this sort of workout be done during the strength phase only so that it becomes a **part** of our system — not a whole system of its own.

Here are examples of training distribution during the strength phase — 5 training days weekly.

intensive period 5, and in some cases even 6, days' work is required each week. For example, in a 6 day stint it would be something like this — 3 days lifting, 1 day fitness (road work etc.), 2 days lifting, 1 day rest. In a 5 workout week it would be — work 3, rest 1, work 2, rest 1. This is the way to progress. In the first month the poundages work up to 70-80 per cent of the maximums, in the second month 80-90 per cent and third 90-100 per cent. Under the Hungarian system this is repeated 4 times during the year so that there are 4 easy months, 4 medium months and 4 months of really hard workouts — all spaced well

Example 1

Monday	— Schedule A
Tuesday	— Rest
Wednesday	— Schedule B
Thursday	— Walking or running or swimming or squash, etc.
Friday	— Schedule A
Saturday	— Schedule B
Sunday	— Rest

Example 2

Monday	— Swim, walk, run
Tuesday	— Schedule A
Wednesday	— Rest
Thursday	— Schedule B
Friday	— Rest
Saturday	— Schedule A
Sunday	— Schedule B

We believe Example 1 gives better, more evenly spread, training and also Sunday with the family. Example 2 gives good hard weekend workouts which many lifters like and leaves Friday, a popular night out, free. The social side is pandered to a little here but to get anywhere lifters **must** be dedicated. The suggestions made will not detract from our aims.

In our phased plan it is suggested that phase 2 be fitness and strength and phase 3 be strength and skill. I recommend that you try the following four workouts or variations on these. Schedules A and B are for strength and power mainly. In Schedules C and D, which are almost identical to the Hungarian schedules, you will see that the Olympic lifts themselves now feature strongly. All four routines are, of course, split workouts with Schedules A and B working alternately; in the following phase Schedules C and D are worked alternately.

Schedule A

Heave jerks	4 sets 5 repetitions
Snatch pulls	3 pulls then 1 to arms' length with dips. Repeat 3 sets of this
Jerks from racks	Work to top training poundage with jumps of 10kg, 7kg, 5kg, 5kg. Repetitions as follows — 4 + 3 + 2 + 1 (top training poundage should be around 90 per cent of top competitive best)
Halting dead lifts	4 sets of 3 repetitions
Hyperextensions	3 sets of 10 repetitions

Schedule B

Wide grip press behind neck	3 sets 3 repetitions, 2 sets 2 repetitions, 3 singles
Snatch balance exercise	4 sets 5 repetitions
Squat cleans	4 sets 5 repetitions
Hang snatch	3 sets 6 repetitions
Front squat or lunge squat	3 sets 6 repetitions

Schedule C

	1st month	2nd month	3rd month
Heave jerks	100 × 5	115 × 3	130 × 3
	120 × 5	135 × 3	155 × 3
	140 × 5	160 × 3	175 × 3
	115 × 5	125 × 3	140 × 3
Power snatch	60 × 3	65 × 3	75 × 3
	85 × 3	85 × 3	95 × 3
	95 × 3	105 × 3	115 × 3
	75 × 3	85 × 3	95 × 3
Clean and jerk	110 × 3	130 × 2	150 × 2
(one jerk only)	130 × 3	150 × 2	170 × 2
	150 × 3	170 × 2	190 × 2
	120 × 3	130 × 2	170 × 2
High pulls	110 × 3	130 × 2	150 × 2
(close grip)	130 × 3	150 × 2	170 × 2
	150 × 3	170 × 2	190 × 2
	120 × 3	130 × 2	170 × 2
Front squat (each workout)	5 light	5 medium	5 heavy

Body bending exercise — done slowly — light and medium resistance only, 8 + 8.

Schedule D

	1st month	2nd month	3rd month
Press behind neck	120 × 5	140 × 3	145 × 3
	95 × 5	115 × 3	120 × 3
	90 × 5	95 × 3	110 × 3
	100 × 5	115 × 3	135 × 3
Snatch	80 × 3	95 × 3	105 × 3
	100 × 3	115 × 3	125 × 3
	120 × 3	135 × 3	145 × 3
	90 × 3	105 × 3	115 × 3
Power clean	100 × 3	115 × 3	130 × 3
	120 × 3	135 × 3	155 × 3
	140 × 3	160 × 3	175 × 3
	115 × 3	125 × 3	140 × 3
High pull (wide grip)	60 × 3	65 × 3	75 × 3
	85 × 3	85 × 3	95 × 3
	95 × 3	105 × 3	115 × 3
	75 × 3	85 × 3	95 × 3
Upward jumps	5 light	5 medium	5 heavy
Abdominal raise	Sets of 5 with 5-10kg		

In a scheme with around 3 months' consecutive skill and strength training, I suggest 2 cycles of 6 weeks divided as follows for these 2 schedules:

75-80 per cent = 2 weeks
85-95 per cent = 2 weeks
90-100 per cent = 2 weeks

The following 6 weeks will have all poundages stepped up from the first 6 weeks. Using the original maximums, the percentage will now be nearer this:

80-85 per cent = 2 weeks
85-95 per cent = 2 weeks
95-100 per cent or 105 per cent
= 2 weeks

The final stage will really be pushing you. Do not be tempted to work hard on weeks where I have suggested only 75-85 per cent. Build up reserves for weeks where you

Doug Hepburn of Canada. Crippled by polio, he overcame his handicap with the help of assistance exercises, technique training and his own determination. He went on to become World Champion

High pulls	70 per cent × 5
	80 per cent × 4
	90 per cent × 4
	95 per cent × 3
	100 per cent × 2
	100 per cent × 1
Power cleans	60 per cent of best power clean 5 + 5
	70 per cent 5 + 5
	80 per cent 5 + 5
	85 per cent 1 + 1
Halting dead lift	100 per cent of best clean. Hold for 4-6 secs then pull as high and fast as possible, 2 pulls 110-115 per cent—ditto
Isometric pulls	Bar at knee height—1 pull 8 secs
	Bar at mid-thigh—1 pull 8 secs
	Bar at top of pull—bar halfway between crutch and belt height. Body fully extended—8 secs

are working to over 90 per cent.

It is during the strength phases that you should aim at correcting weaknesses. If your pull needs improving, this is the time to work on it. Perhaps your overhead work is weak — if so, emphasise exercises to correct it.

This is the period when you will use racks, overhead chains for supporting and so on.

If you wish to improve your pulling power, some exercises and suggested percentages of your best snatch and clean are given above. All pulls should be done with straps.

Phase 3 — Strength and skill

As before there is an overlapping of the phases. There was some lifting in the fitness phase, some fitness work in the strength phase. We saw that the Olympics figured in Schedules C and D of the strength phase and you will find that there is still a lot of

George Hilley trains on high pulls

assistance work in the skill phase.

It should be noted, however, that there are some vital differences plus a change of emphasis. The Olympic lifts in Schedules C and D involved sets of three to five repetitions. This is not particularly good for building movement patterns and good technique, so as training moves into a more advanced stage repetitions are decreased and there are many twos and singles. Once again the 'pyramid' figures in our scheme of work. Within our overall pyramid we now have a little pyramid of repetitions — 4 repetitions + 3 repetitions + 2 repetitions + 1 repetition is a common training concept.

This of course means that during this phase there will be a decrease of total tonnage but an increase in intensity. The tonnage will still be fairly high but as you move towards the peak the total work volume must take second place to intensity. In other words low repetitions must be arrived at, even if there is a decrease in total work. We must consider that the total is made up of only two lifts, the best snatch and best clean and jerk. The winner may not be the one with the best average on the six lifts, in fact his average may be very poor. We are, in the final analysis, concerned only with two maximum intensity efforts.

To reach this, a fantastic volume of training must be done. All my studies on the subject seem to indicate that a plan which makes a progressive development from a wide basis of fitness to a very narrow basis of intensity is the most productive system and if we use this as a guide in every phase, it results in a logical system which gives the necessary stamina, speed, strength and finally skill.

The skill and strength phase is one of the most critical not only from a physical point of view but mentally too. The strength phase is extremely important and probably the one which will make the greatest difference in totals from year to year. For this reason instead of a clear cut division between the skill and strength phases we prefer a very 'blurred' border where there is still a lot of strength work being done **but with a shifting of emphasis.** The coach should now be stressing the more correct path of movement in assistance work. I am not insinuating that pulls, etc. should be done as skill training but the lifter must try to see that instead of building power alone he aims for **correct application of this power.** For example, in pulling exercises he will set his knees under the bar and try to sweep the hips slightly forward and upwards instead of 'counter-balancing' by moving the shoulders and back round the hips which stay in the same place. In the front squat the feet will be placed exactly as they would be in rising from the clean; snatch balance exercises are ideal at this stage of training as they include an element of related skill as well as strength.

It is all a question of keeping priorities in mind by shifting the emphasis. New training patterns will emerge although the schedule may not be greatly altered. The actual competitive lifts must be the most important exercises here, and they must all be practised intensively each week in addition to the numerous power movements. This means that in the early stages you may have three different workouts to be done each week. The clean and jerk may in this case be treated as two lifts. A different competitive lift should have priority each session.

Excellent results have been achieved by the following regime in this final phase of training.

a. **3 days training + 1 day rest + 2 days training**

b. **2 days training + 1 day rest + 2 days training**

c. **Alternate days training**

d. **Tapering off period**

If you are working on a two cycle plan this will result in a, b, c and d being divided roughly as follows — 14 days, 12 days, 13 days and 6 days. In a single cycle plan (a) would take approximately five weeks, (b) 4 weeks, (c) 3 weeks of alternate day training, (d) tapering off and contest 5 days, then one week's rest.

We have pointed out the necessity for heavier weights and lower repetitions even if it means lessening the total amount of work. It could be argued that if it is easier to build strength and muscular endurance, etc. with heavy weights done for five or six repetitions then this should be continued. This system would work but we have seen that lower repetitions — singles and twos — work even better for several reasons. High on the list is the fact that there is a psychological urge to handle heavy weights approximating to competition efforts as the contest approaches. Secondly, it is a fact that lifts with light or medium weights **do not repeat the patterns which are done with top weights no matter how skilled the lifter may be.** In case this fact is disputed let me repeat the findings reported by the Russian researcher Arootunyan in **Theory and Practice of Physical Culture** (1964). This was an analysis of dynamograms and mechano-grams of lifters doing the fast lifts. The tests were on a wide variety of subjects — 14 of good club level, 36 first class lifters and 32 Masters of Sport, which in the USSR means good international standard. The investigations recorded 2,460 lifts. There were five snatches and five jerks per subject with weights of 60-65 per cent maximum, 70-75, 80-85, 90-95 and 100 per cent. Each of the five lifts was performed one time every three to five minutes.

His findings were most interesting. The study of the jerk showed that with the heaviest weights, the movement pattern was much more stereotyped: 'there is a strong and deeper stereotype of movement, **which does not appear with lesser weights**' (the emphasis is mine).

Where the poundage was 70-75 and 80-85 per cent maximum, there were different results in distribution of effort. There appeared to be a 'braking' in the lift which was not present when the competitor used top weights, although the best lifters could repeat the movement pattern more accurately with the lower weights than the lesser lifters could. Arootunyan concluded that this showed that the Masters of Sport and first class athletes had better developed 'muscular feel', or what our sports technicians would term 'kinesthetic sense'. The second and third class lifters had the proper stereotyping only in the heavier weights. These

remarks deal with the jerk but the same picture was seen in the snatch. In top lifters the 75-85 per cent weights do not permit the best technique and tempo. **It is highly recommended that for perfection the lifters must work up to maximum and near maximum weights during training.**

I am indebted to the late John P. Jesse for the detailed information about this research as it shows how thoroughly the Russians treated the subject and one can have confidence in the validity of the research.

Poundages in assistance work

In this phase you can use poundages which are actually higher than your best efforts in similar Olympic lifts, e.g. snatch and clean pulls. Not more than 5 repetitions should be done and most likely, with such heavy lifts, poundages will be less and the accent on sets rather than repetitions. Around 5-8 sets are common but seldom, if ever, should you go above 10 sets.

In such assistance work you should consider 90-100 per cent of a similar Olympic movement as a medium-heavy weight; anything under 70 per cent would be light.

These different loads are specifically mentioned as

lifting must not continue with heavy loads exclusively in spite of what has been said earlier regarding skill training. If you continue to push the 80-95 per cent poundages you will go stale very quickly. Over-training is a great problem for dedicated trainees. A number of enthusiasts are scared to drop poundages in case they lose the progress they have made, but in fact it is by **not** dropping that they will go 'stale'.

Whether on assistance work or Olympics you **must** ease off every two or three weeks (the Russians advise a drop after 6-7 sessions, that is about two weeks' training under their system).

There is one final point about poundages and repetitions in this phase which relates to the total tonnage used. We have stressed the need for increasing intensity but we must be careful that the tonnage is not increased too much. The problem need not resolve itself into merely juggling with repetitions and poundages, for a further aspect which must not be overlooked is that the **number of exercises can also be cut.** This will allow increased poundages without decreased volume in that schedule when this is felt desirable.

Some skill phase schedules

In all the following schedules the poundages and increases depend a great deal on your personal standard. A world champion might start 90kg under his top lift but if you only do 70kg on the same lift then obviously you must adapt the poundages and increases accordingly. The suggestions provide a fairly average guide.

There is a different workout for each training session per week, e.g. Monday, Wednesday, Friday and Sunday. It is suggested that heavy try-outs be on Sundays.

Workout 1

Heave jerks: Dip at start and finish, no foot movement. Start approximately 30kg below top. Work up in 5kg jumps as follows — 3 + 3 + 2 + 2 + singles to top training weight. Follow with 2-3 singles with this. Drop 12kg — 1 single. Add 5kg — 1 single.
Snatch start: 30kg below starting poundage. Do sets of 3s and 2s working up in 5-7½kg jumps to top. Do several singles (maximum 6) with top training poundages.

Front squats: 3 sets of 5 repetitions: light — medium — heavy.
Cleans from hang: 4 + 3 + 2 + 2 + 1 + 1.
Sit ups: 3 sets of 8 repetitions. Weight behind neck.

Workout 2

Power snatch and snatch: The procedure here is to power snatch the first few sets. When you need to dip, start full snatches on the next set. Do 6 to 7 sets of 2 repetitions plus 3-6 singles, increasing weight each set. Do 2 singles with top training weight.
Halting dead lift (straps): Hold for 5 seconds minimum then pull as high and fast as possible. Repeat twice only.
Roman chair sit ups: Weight at chest 3 + 3 + 2 + 1.
3 standing long jumps + 3 jumps to touch board.

Workout 3

Cleans: 3 + 3 + 2 + 2 + 1 + 1 + 1 increasing poundages. Drop 10kg.
1 clean and jerk. Add 5-7 ½ kg. 1 clean and jerk.
Heave and sink in split position: 5 sets of 2 repetitions + 5 singles, increasing poundages in all sets.
High pulls (snatch grip): 4-6 sets of 3 repetitions increasing weight in first 3 sets only.
Front squats or lunge squats: 3-5 repetitions: light — medium — heavy.
Snatch balance exercise: 3 + 3 + 3 + 2 + 2 + 4-6 singles increasing in all sets except singles.
Sit ups: Several sets of 10 repetitions. Weight behind neck.

Workout 4

100 up (run on spot): 100 knee lifts, fast as possible for last 20.
Jerks from racks: 3 + 2 + 3 + 2 + 5-8 singles going as high as possible. Every effort should be made to go well above best clean.
Snatches: 3 + 3 + 2 + 3 singles, to approximately 85-90 per cent of best.
Push press: 4 + 3 + 2 + 1 + 1 + 1 increasing each set.
Roman chair sit ups: As Workout 2.

Special pre-contest preparation

In order to prepare the lifter for competition conditions there should be some attention to varying **training** conditions as the contest approaches. The lifter should accustom himself to different views. In the club he is usually on the same spot facing the same way all the time. In competition he may be put off by the size of the hall, or merely because it looks different. The Iron Curtain countries are great believers in changing training conditions in club, facing lifters sometimes

George Hilley: front squats

the opposite way and when possible working out in a different place. This sort of variation can be carried further. Sometimes at contests the competitor is called to lift before he is fully warmed up or else before he is mentally prepared. At other times, because of failures by previous lifters and further attempts at the same weight, he may be delayed more than anticipated. This could upset lifters. In Kiselev's work on training for competitive conditions he advises variations in **timing** between lifts and even during the lifts. Thus confidence can be built and the lifter develops the ability to go early or late in competition without an adverse effect. Taking this to the ultimate, the pauses at the chest in the clean and jerk can be varied in case of an unsettling action in the clean.

Finally, the increases between attempts should sometimes be varied for similar reasons to those mentioned. A few variations go a long way so once the principle has been established and included periodically, guard against overdoing it. It is most effective in the later stages of the skill phase — don't waste it!

Tapering off

This is of tremendous importance and a fairly clear pattern can be observed during the preparation for major international tournaments although there are notable exceptions to this procedure. Suffice to say that this is in keeping with the methods adopted by the winners of current world titles. When calculating tapering off schedules, I prefer to work backwards from the contest as this helps to put the system into clearer perspective.

The last two days should be rest. This does not mean lying in bed all day but there should not be any more hard work or even long walks. The most that should be done is a little strolling around in a **restful atmosphere** — not in busy places or shopping centres. A few mobility exercises are permissible but these should be of a gentle stretching nature rather than vigorous.

The last workout should be two days before the contest and you can snatch to **almost** starting poundages — work up to 5-10kg below your first effort on the platform. Anything else done during the workout should be of a 'tinkering' nature and with light weights.

For all tapering off workouts, and the last few full workouts, all lifting should be timed to assess the minimum recovery time needed between warming up lifts so that you can accurately time your pre-contest preparation at the event. It is also recommended that the pre-contest limbering up free exercises and light weight warming up routine be included in the last dozen or so workouts. The third and fourth days before the contest will include medium workouts where the total tonnage is quite low but the individual poundages are of medium intensity. Starting poundages must **not** be tried but there may well be singles with poundages approaching these.

The fifth day before the contest is the last chance to try really heavy poundages and the aim should be to go right up to starting poundages; if this goes well, some extra attempts may be made. This should be the last attempt to better starting poundages on this lift. Jerks from the rack, however, may be done with top training weights. Heavy singles are needed to work to a peak and a lifter peaking too slowly can have the peak brought forward by more heavy singles — likewise guard against too many, as this will put a lifter over the top of a peak. Singles take much more out of you mentally than repetitions, a fact which must not be overlooked in planning recovery times and workouts.

It is permissible to do quite a

lengthy workout and include some light squats and pulls in addition to the competitive lifts but this is the last occasion on which these will be done. Make sure that straps are used for the pull as research has shown that the grip 'drops off' considerably with effort and a reserve of strength should be built as competition day approaches.

These are the vital days before the match and the true tapering off period. The sixth day before the contest should be a rest day, unless for some reason (such as travel arrangements) the tapering off procedure outlined has to be adjusted.

Flexibility in lifting

Because weightlifting has traditionally an image of strength and power, and being a sport which attracts men who are well endowed with these characteristics, other very necessary physical attributes are apt to be overlooked. Clearly, power is of prime importance; the need for speed and agility in the two classic lifts is also recognised and training should be geared accordingly. It is my belief, however, that the need for **flexibility** is still very much neglected. Shoulder mobility, of course, is a very obvious necessity for squat style lifters, but that is where many people stop.

They see the importance of supple shoulders but overlook the necessity for supple back, hips, knees and ankle joints. Modern lifters **must** regularly work every major joint through its full range, with active and passive stretching of the muscle groups. Similar exercises should also be an integral part of every warming up programme as this will have a beneficial effect on subsequent lifting. A full and detailed description of the many interesting and advantageous mobility exercises is outside the scope of this book, but it is well within our present remit to draw attention to the advantages of good flexibility and the results of a lack of suppleness.

If shoulder mobility is lacking, the chances of holding the bar correctly and comfortably overhead in maximum attempts is greatly reduced and the failure rate greatly increased. A supple spinal column will allow the upper back to be vertical although the lower part of the spine is not directly under the weight, so spinal mobility is essential.

The person with good flexibility of ankles, knees and hips will be able to assume a very good low position to receive the weights; some junior lifters give fine examples

Get your heels down! This lifter's raised heels reduce the size of his base, making the lift less stable. Raised heels can be caused by lack of ankle flexibility or an unbalanced lift

of what can be done with good mobility.

The need for mobile ankles is not well-known and needs greater attention. The ability to steeply incline the shins forward, well in advance of the toes, gives a much better position by reducing the tilt of the pelvis, which in turn reduces the lumbar curve.

Those who have not got this flexibility resort to compensating manoeuvres, often unaware that they are doing so. Typical of these is the device where the feet are spread wide and toes turned out as the lifter goes into the low squat. Both these manoeuvres have the effect of reducing the size of the lifter's base so lack of flexibility of the ankle joint reduces his chances of success. Adding a higher heel to the lifting boot, as some lifters do, is not the answer as this prevents the lifter from fully utilising his strength — for example, it reduces the amount of work which can be done by the calf (gastrocnemius) muscles during the pull.

An old-fashioned fault, now largely eradicated, was the tight lacing of high-ankle boots designed to support the ankle joint. Far from helping the lifter this restricted ankle movement and it is significant that the disappearance of high-ankled boots coincided with the popular emergence of modern squat lifting. While ankle mobility is necessary in split lifting this style is not so demanding except on the ankle of the forward foot during a snatch.

This short résumé is only an example of how flexibility of a single body part can affect competitive lifts and I have deliberately chosen the ankles to illustrate the point as they have a less obvious connection with the snatch than do the shoulders or back. It is hoped that all lifters will accept the view that joint mobility is of considerable importance and will include flexibility exercises as an integral part of their training programme.

Bibliography

There is a dearth of modern literature on competitive weightlifting. (This is why I have written this book!) Some of the books still being sold cover the press, which was dropped after the 1972 Olympic Games. Many of the following books are out of print, but I include them for historical interest to show how the sport and training developed.

British Amateur Weight Lifters Association, *Instructor's Handbook* (updated periodically)

Halliday, Jim, *Olympic Weightlifting* (Pullum & Son, London, 1950)

Hoffman, Bob, *Weightlifting* (Strength & Health Publishing Co, 1939)

Inch, Thomas, *The Art and Science of Lifting* (Mendip Press, 1903)

International Weightlifting Federation, *Constitution and Rule Book* (updated periodically)

Kirkley, George, *Modern Weightlifting* (Faber Popular Books, 1957)

Lambert, Georges, *Halterophile* (Editions Vigot, Paris, 1978)

Lear, John, *EP Sport Weightlifting* (EP Publishing, 1980)

Mihajlovic, Vladan, *80 Years of Weightlifting* (IWF, Belgrade, 1977)

Murray, Alistair, *Modern Weight Training* (Kaye & Ward, 1971)

Popplewell, George, *Modern Weightlifting and Power Lifting* (Faber, 1978)

Pullum, W A, *Weightlifting Made Easy and Interesting* (Athletic Publications Limited, c. 1935)

Saxon, Arthur, *The Textbook of Weightlifting* (Health and Strength Limited, c. 1910)

Tikrity, Wadie Y, *Weightlifting Theory and Practice* (Iraq, 1985)

Vorobyev, Dr Arcady, *Weightlifting* (IWF, Budapest, 1977)

Webster, David, *Defying Gravity* (D P Webster, 1964) (Revised and republished as *The Two Hands Snatch* (Iron Man Publications, USA)

Webster, David, *The Development of the Clean and Jerk* (Iron Man Publications, 1966)

Webster, David, *The Iron Game: an illustrated history of weightlifting* (D P Webster, 1976)

Wright, Russell, *The Making of an Olympic Champion* (Exposition Press, New York, 1976)